DATE DUE

Demco, Inc. 38-293

Divided Countries, Separated Cities

Divided Countries, Separated Cities

The Modern Legacy of Partition

edited by

Ghislaine Glasson Deschaumes
and
Rada Iveković

OXFORD
UNIVERSITY PRESS

54372881

12-18-06

OXFORD
UNIVERSITY PRESS

YMCA Library Building, Jai Singh Road, New Delhi 110 001

Oxford University Press is a department of the University of Oxford. It furthers the University's objective of excellence in research, scholarship, and education by publishing worldwide in

Oxford   New York

Auckland   Bangkok   Buenos Aires   Cape Town   Chennai
Dar es Salaam   Delhi   Hong Kong   Istanbul   Karachi   Kolkata
Kuala Lumpur   Madrid   Melbourne   Mexico City   Mumbai   Nairobi
São Paulo   Shanghai   Taipei   Tokyo   Toronto

Oxford is a registered trade mark of Oxford University Press
in the UK and in certain other countries

Published in India
By Oxford University Press, New Delhi

Divided Countries, Separated Cities © Oxford University Press, 2003
Individual articles © *Transeuropéennes*

The moral rights of the author have been asserted
Database right Oxford University Press (maker)

First published winter 2000–2001
As *Transeuropéennes* Numéro 19/20

ISBN 0 19 566540 6

Typeset in Goudy 10/12.9
By Jojy Philip New Delhi 110 027
Printed by Pauls Press, New Delhi 110 020
Published by Manzar Khan, Oxford University Press
YMCA Library Building, Jai Singh Road, New Delhi 110 001

Contents

Preface

They are accepted as warding off still longer conflicts, and preventing genocide. At some precise, yet often obscure, moment in the contentious event, they are presented as the only possible response to the desire for war between the communities or ideologies involved. Partition processes are set into motion in situations where transaction is lacking—is caused to be lacking. They signal the failure of politics and of 'civility' (E. Balibar, *Transeuropéennes* no. 18). For nearly a century, partition has been a mode of conflict withdrawal. Yet, can it really provide a long-term solution to a conflict? Prevent further conflicts? What, in other words, is the taste of peace brought on by division? What is the taste of life in cities that have been separated, cleft in two, where division invariably entails the utmost violence being inflicted on bodies, minds, and modes of being together?

For seven years now, *Transeuropéennes* has sought to engage in critical thinking regarding processes of fragmentation and exclusion, identity-based violence, the impulses behind displacement and exile, as well as on processes of coming together, politics, and figures of civility. By putting these contradictory dynamics into perspective within the historical event of partition, this volume is a culmination point. At the same time, through the new questions it raises regarding the ongoing interaction between divisions and globalizations, on the meaning of those states of peace which stem from these processes, it is an invitation to question our present with both acuity and vigilance.

It is an open question as to whether or not the Partition of India constitutes a paradigm case. And indeed the question is debated in this volume. At any rate, through its very scope, the feeling it gives of remaining still unfinished, its impact on the day-to-day political life of South Asia, and the trauma it has brought with it, as well as the knowledge it has produced over the past several years in the field of historiography, political philosophy, and the sociology of migrations, the Partition of India stands out as an indispensable and instructive reference for equipping our thinking on the partition processes underway in Europe and elsewhere in the world. Thanks is thus due to the authors—and the translators—of this issue, who encouraged and supported this comparative proposition and the aspiration to question the state of peace to which partition gives rise.

As will be seen, division is not stability. By questioning attempts at conflict resolution through processes of partition, *Transeuropéennes* has sought to look both to the past and to the future, thus posing the question in terms of time and space. The space of partition seems better known: that of the physical and mental, visible and invisible border, swiftly internalized once established.

It is the old land split up; the native village transformed into a foreign and inaccessible land; the same transformed into the other. The border polarizes the new national identities, upholding them by hindering any new 'fray' (J.-L. Nancy, *Transeuropéennes* no. 1) between populations, between differences. Closed off in most cases, borders are sufficiently permeable to enable the trafficking of people and goods. And sufficiently sealed that social and family ties cannot be rewoven.

The time of partition is more elusive, and a number of the texts in this issue help us to grasp its framework. Pre-partition is the time of the stigmatization of communities, of rising tensions around projects seeking to demonstrate the incompatibility of the collective identities involved, whether they be religious, linguistic, ideological, or economic, and the laborious interference—or intercession, depending on the case—of the international powers that be. Pre-partition is subsequently presented as the enigmatic moment when the political path was abandoned in favour of the logic of division and separation—as the point where everything toppled once and for all. How, while there is still time, is the separation of forces to prevail over that of human beings?

The moment of partition itself is the time of collective violence against individual destinies, that of massacres, the rape of women, aiming at wresting the other from the self, aiming at an unlikely homogeneity. It is the time of forced individual and mass displacements, the time when the refugee becomes the emblematic figure in the process (*see Transeuropéennes* no. 12/13). Displaced persons are no longer in coincidence with their surroundings: having become foreigners where they were, they then become foreign bodies in the community to which they have come on the other side of the border. Through their doubly impossible existence in their place of origin and in their place of arrival in the wake of partition, these people, doubly displaced—in time and in space—are amputated from their own biographies.

After partition, the time of partition continues to prevail. It invades the present and mortgages the future, structuring mentalities, modes of representation, around a before and an after, which, upon closer examination, turn out to be blurry zones indeed. After partition, partition never seems able to end. It is the time of the pressing question, so often raised in *Transeuropéennes*, and to which a number of authors return: 'How are representations of the past and the future to be decommunitarized?'

PROLOGUE

Settling Partition Hostilities
Lessons Learnt, the Options Ahead

RADHA KUMAR

One aim of this paper is to draw up a checklist of the lessons learnt from the successes and/or failures of older partitions for the debate on present-day policy options in ongoing ethnic conflicts; the other is to see what light these shed on current partition-related peace processes.

With this question in mind, I chose to look at a set of cases comprising both colonial and post-Cold War ethnic partitions. In a Council on Foreign Relations study group, I have examined the partition theory from its disparate roots in British colonialism and Wilsonian self-determination, to its latter-day protagonists, and have conducted a case by case examination of the partition conflicts in Ireland, India-Pakistan, Israel-Palestine, Cyprus, and the former Yugoslavia. This article attempts a broad summary of the lessons derived from these sessions, and a checklist of the best and worst case options available to the international community.

Since the Dayton Peace Agreement of November 1995, which brought an end to the Bosnian war, there has been increasing debate on whether or not partition can provide a solution to ethnic conflict, either in the short or in the long term. The Yugoslav wars and the Serb-Albanian divide, the renewed hostilities between Ethiopia and Eritrea, north and south Sudan, and north-east and south-west Sri Lanka, have all made the issue of secession and/or partition of critical interest to international policy in a post-Cold War world. In a way similar to the sharp breaks which prevailed at the time of the League of Nations and just after World War II, international policy is once again debating the stand-off between territorial integrity and self-determination, with the emerging doctrine of humanitarian action as a kind of fuzzy middle ground, as yet unready to tackle the 'what next?' questions of final status. Established partitions such as India-Pakistan and East Timor, volatile partitions such as Northern Ireland and Cyprus, and partitions-in-the-making such as Israel-Palestine, Bosnia-Herzegovina and—doubtfully—Kosovo, are of especial interest here, for both the retrospective and contemporary lessons they offer. In each case, too, there is an ongoing or attempted peace process which reflects the emerging view that stability and the prevention of future conflict might be best achieved through either re-unifying partitioned areas, or settling their more hostile legacies.

Initially, the partition debate suffered from a lack of clarity on what distinguished ethnic partitions from other ethnic conflicts, partly because ethnic conflicts and resulting partitions had not been studied from the standpoint of policy-making. The bulk of the existing literature belongs in the category of history or official reports. Much of the discussion, moreover, has been restricted to individual partitions rather than the policy lessons they might offer when looked at in reference to one another. A case-by-case approach has continued to dominate partition studies. But whereas almost every leading think-tank or foreign-policy school has conducted studies on India–Pakistan, Israel–Palestine, Cyprus, and Bosnia, in which partition provided a context (if not, in general, the chief point of study), rarely have studies on one area referred to those on another, even when borrowing models for negotiation or settlement. The result, frequently, is that proposed alternatives tend to be unvarying despite time and situation changes and therefore have mixed policy impact.

In the wake of the Dayton Agreement, however, a debate has sprung up on partition policy per se. Interestingly, the contemporary pro-partition advocates adopt the received wisdom of British colonial arguments for partition, rather than the Wilsonian formulae for self-determination. The colonial argument advocated the creation of ethnically-based states through territorial partition as a lesser evil to what they predicted could be potential genocide. In practice, though, partition was used as an exit strategy (in the now famous words of the British historian and civil servant, Penderel Moon, a policy of 'divide and quit'), rather than being based on any consideration of the needs and desires of the people affected. In a post-colonial and post-Cold War period, however, it is not clear whether partition can work either as a lesser evil or as an exit strategy.

Lessons Learnt: Partition as a Solution

Far from providing a solution to ethnic conflict, partition aims have been an underlying element in the descent to war, and have more often served to stimulate strife rather than to end it. Indeed, negotiations towards partition have paralleled, and most often foreshadowed, war: partition as an alternative to devolution was discussed in Ireland in 1912, but took ten years and a civil war to be achieved, in 1922; India suffered a first partition, in Bengal, in 1905, and partition was on the table from 1940 onwards, but was established only in 1947, when it was accompanied by an ethnic conflict in which between 500,000 to a million people died and over fifteen million were displaced. In Palestine, partition was first proposed by the Peel Commission in 1937, and then again by the UN in 1948, but was subsumed by wars which began with the expulsion of a large proportion of Palestinians from what is now Israel. It ended with Israel's establishment and the occupation of the West Bank and Golan Heights, only to re-emerge in the context of the Oslo peace process, which is focused on the question of a partition of the West Bank. In Cyprus, partition was threatened in 1956, avoided in 1960, and reappeared through a ten-year ethnic conflict ending with Turkey's invasion in 1974 and the de facto partition of the island. The still putative partition of Bosnia-Herzegovina took almost four years of war to arrive at and continues to simmer under five years of peace, while Kosovo's partition is being discussed in what can at best be described as a boiling peace, coming in the wake of more than a decade of conflict which culminated in the NATO bombing campaign of spring 1999. Because demography is crucial in defining partitions, they rarely succeed in satisfying aspirations towards self-determination. The attempt to draw ethnic borders around populations which are, as President Izetbegović put it in the first year of the Bosnian war, as intermingled as corn and flour, generally leads to ethnic cleansing and leaves beleaguered enclaves within contested borders. In this sense, partition incites ancient hatreds rather than settling them. Indeed, the contest over setting new borders tends to restructure the sources of ethnic conflict, and burdens the international system with the permanent threat of war. Israel remains the only state with undeclared borders; Kashmir has been a bone of contention between India and Pakistan since partition; and the international community's attempt to evade the partition question in Bosnia by giving Brcko autonomous status has turned the district into a microcosm of the 'now you see it, now you don't' partition of Bosnia.

By contrast, it is easier for negotiated secessions or dissolved federations to succeed. Czechoslovakia could negotiate a 'velvet divorce' because the two states were relatively homogenous, and therefore their separation did not involve the forced migration of Czechs and Slovaks. (The implications of this are that it ought to be easier for relatively homogenous areas, such as East Timor or North Sudan, to separate. The fact that bitter wars have been fought over them, instead, only puts the onus more squarely on the undemocratic state.) A corresponding point—that war and forced migration could be avoided by population transfers—begs the following points: (a) population transfers will still require force and carry the threat of conflict; (b) they require international intervention; and (c) they are subject to questions of scale. Is it possible to imagine any agency—other than a xenophobic one—which could undertake to transfer the roughly sixteen-million people affected by the Indian partition?

Most recently, the idea of population transfers has arisen in the Kosovo conflict: that the Albanians of southern Serbia move to northern Kosovo, and the Serbs in northern Kosovo move to southern Serbia. Apart from the fact that there is little evidence to show that the two communities would voluntarily move, the proposal would appear to fetishize existing borders—why not adjust Kosovo's borders instead? And while it is presumably intended to avoid setting a precedent about changing republican borders, it could send a dangerous message both to Bosnia (that the effects of ethnic cleansing can be legitimized as a population transfer), and to Macedonia (that working towards a multi-ethnic democracy is not a winning proposition). Indeed, the proposal draws attention to a related problem in ethnic conflicts, that of states with contiguous diasporas. These can either extend conflict, as in Bosnia with the Croats on one side and the Serbs on the other, and Cyprus with the Greeks on one side and the Turks on the other (separated though both are by the sea). Or they can indefinitely prolong it, as between India and Pakistan over the Kashmir.

Partitioned lands tend to remain in a long-term situation of flux in which both collective and individual insecurity are sensitive even to minor irritants and thus conflict erupts frequently. Whether de jure or de facto, ethnic partitions have not stabilized over time. Conflict in Northern Ireland has lasted seventy years and spawned a prolonged phase of terrorism; the fifty-year-long hostility between India and Pakistan has devolved on Kashmir (also leading, along the way, to the creation of Bangladesh); Greece and Turkey have several times come close to threatening war over Cyprus while the Green Line remains a zone of tension; conflict over Israel and Palestine continues to this day. Despite five years of peace, Bosnia remains so volatile that countries contributing peace-keeping troops all fear that any attempt to withdraw might result in the renewal of war. The spectre hovering over discussions of a Kosovo partition includes the spread of conflict in south Serbia and Macedonia. Most recently, India and Pakistan's nuclear tests of 1998 have acquired an especially dangerous edge because of the ongoing and escalating conflict in Kashmir.

A further cause of instability is that ethnic partitions tend to usher in relatively undemocratic states, or undemocratic enclaves within democracies. Pakistan and Bangladesh have had more years under military than civilian rule; northern Cyprus is dominated by an alliance between the Turkish army and a local suzerain, Mr Rauf Denktash; Israel's occupation of the West Bank and Gaza, Lebanon and the Golan Heights, made it a pariah until the Oslo process began. Britain's advanced democracy lived with the uneasy fact of being a brutal presence in Northern Ireland until the Framework Agreements; India's developing democracy lives equally uneasily with its gross violation of human rights in Kashmir. Xenophobia is alive in Bosnia and Kosovo.

The international community has so far accepted the instability of ethnic partitions because their primary purpose has been to provide an exit strategy or a means of limited containment rather than a lasting solution to an ethnic conflict. Partition worked as an exit strategy during the colonial period because it could be accepted as the price of independence. Self-determination movements in Ireland, India, and—in a skewed fashion—Palestine (the Zionists alone), swallowed the bitter pill of partition as a necessary evil in the greater good of statehood and/or decolonization. During the Cold War, partition acted as means of containment, or the delineation of spheres of influence. Though this applied primarily to ideological partitions, as in Germany, Vietnam, and Korea, ethnic partitions were sheltered by its rubric and were treated as a means of limited containment: the British army's fiat in Northern Ireland was justified as at least keeping the level of violence down, while the de facto partition of Cyprus was viewed as circumscribing the limits of a stand-off between Greece and Turkey.

In a post-colonial and post-Cold War world, however, ethnic partitions can no longer be viewed as the price of independence, and so they fail to provide even an exit strategy for great powers or international institutions. Kosovo is a comprehensive example of the nature of the problem: after the

NATO bombing campaign, it would have been impossible for the international community to persuade the Kosovo Albanians that partition was the price of their independence, even if the international community had favoured partition in the first place (for which there is no evidence); independence, however, will not be favoured at present, what with the twin spectres of Montenegrin pressure for independence and intensified ethnic fissures in Macedonia looming. Indeed, in both Bosnia and Kosovo, both local populations and leaderships are actively seeking an international presence in preference to independence. (Of the five cases under study, Palestine is perhaps the only ongoing conflict in which partition—of the West Bank—is being offered as the price of independence. Whether, however, it can be an acceptable price remains to be seen, given its stark injustice, and the many ambiguities surrounding it. Indeed, the territorial negotiations, grim as they are, are outweighed by the literally existential question of Palestinian refugees. As Israel's withdrawal from Lebanon has inadvertently underlined, President Arafat is not in a position to subsume their aspirations, even should he wish to do so).

Moreover, with the end of the bloc system, the development of information technology, and the gradual integration of markets, containment is no longer a viable strategy. While the Yugoslav wars are the most potent example of the dissipation of containment following the end. of the bloc system, its end has also spawned a free movement of arms and a freer—if not new—breed of cross-border and cross-continent conflicts whose chief protagonists are non-state actors. In this context, instead of acting as a putative exit strategy, the adoption of ethnic-partition policies more often constitutes an entry which embroils great powers and international institutions in a long-term and ever extending program of stabilization. As the NATO–UN–EU presence in Bosnia, and the UN administrations in Kosovo and East Timor show, the international community is beginning to recognise that intervention can carry with it the obligation to engage in post-conflict stabilisation, including state-building. Thus far, the international administrations have been hampered by a reluctance both to expand responsibilities and to provide resources. In the beginning, in Bosnia, the international community was unwilling to take on the task of state-building, and thus the immediate post-conflict phase was marked by a stratified, indeed anomic, division of responsibilities between often competing institutions, in which the great loser was the administration (as in state-building), in particular, the rule of law. This lacuna has been partly compensated for in the mandates of the UN administrations of Kosovo and East Timor, though both are plagued by a problem which is also crucial in Bosnia: inadequate aid and manpower compounded by a lag between the pledge of aid and its delivery.

Post-conflict Stabilization and Reconstruction

A major impediment to post-conflict stabilization is that attempts to implement provisions for reconstruction and development, which fail to tackle the central dilemma of partition, can remain hostage to party rivalries. Even in the longer-term post-conflict phase, trade, infrastructure, and demographic or familial interests are unable to undermine or bypass the hostilities of partition without outside stimuli. In Northern Ireland and India, and in the UN partition plan for Palestine, it was assumed that, over time, economic interests would dissolve the partition lines. Instead, partition lines hardened over time, hampering trade, development, and communication. Unofficial trade between India and Pakistan, for example, is conservatively estimated at $2 billion; official trade, in comparison, has rarely exceeded $200 million. And the two countries are, in this respect, better off than most other partitioned lands. Telephone calls between the two parts of Cyprus have to be made through Greece and Turkey, respectively. Indeed, even attempts to use economic incentives to jumpstart partition peace processes, without tackling the central dilemma of partition, have foundered: the EU's cross-border projects for Ireland-Northern Ireland had little effect until the framework agreements began to be implemented, and key areas of the agreements, such as the power-sharing executive, have themselves come close to foundering over the issues of decommissioning and police reform. The Lahore process between India and Pakistan came to an end before it even took off, largely because the military feared that Prime Minister Sharif was willing to abandon Pakistan's Kashmir policy in the interests of expanding the country's exchequer. Cross-border projects are rare in Bosnia and as yet unthinkable in Kosovo; even localized attempts to stimulate economic reconstruction have been hampered by an uncertain political future, in which accountability is one of the first victims. How, after all, do you hold political representatives accountable for corruption in a situation in which you don't know where their responsibility begins and the international administration leaves off— or, for that matter, a situation which teeters between war and peace?

There is now a dawning recognition that trade and development will flower after the central dilemma of partition is tackled, either through reintegration (to differing extents, Cyprus, Bosnia, and Kosovo), or through settling its more hostile legacies (Ireland, India-Pakistan, East Timor). How to move towards these goals, however, remains inchoate, especially because in post-Cold War conflicts such as Bosnia and Kosovo, the key issues of demilitarization and decommissioning, state and civil institution-building, the return of refugees, and economic reconstruction, are overshadowed by the lethal combination of an uncertain political future and international fears of deepening embroilment. Thus, for example, despite its recognition that tackling decommissioning and institution-building is the key to refugee return and reconstruction, the international community's strategy in Bosnia has focused disproportionately on two areas: elections and fiscal reform. Admittedly, neither is easy to tackle in societies which have suffered widespread destruction. By contrast, in the decolonization phase, the degree of destruction caused by the conflict was relatively low (for example, infrastructure was not devastated in the Ireland, India-Pakistan, or Israel-Palestine wars); and there was a legitimate party to take over power, whose business it then was to deal with state-building, refugee issues, and so on. Indeed, reconstruction and state-building are key areas of differentiation between colonial partitions and post-Cold War partition-related conflicts. Historically, where partitions occurred as part of the transfer of power, there were, by and large, legitimate political parties to hand power over to—such as the nationalists in the Irish Republic, the Indian National Congress in India, and the Muslim League in Pakistan. This allowed greater flexibility: for example, paramilitaries disappeared as lawful armies emerged; aid and resources could be offered by diaspora communities, 'parent' nations, or governments sympathetic to the party in power, who might have held back if they had instead been required to deal with an interim international administration. Demilitarization and decommissioning, police and adminis-tration, the establishment of the rule of law, and the development of civil institutions could thus proceed (with hiccups) in Ireland, India, Pakistan, and the Republic of Cyprus. (Where there were no legitimate parties to hand power over to—such as within Northern Ireland or in de facto partition cases, such as Northern Cyprus or in Pakistan-held Azad Kash-mir—state and civil institution-building remained in abeyance, and the areas remained relatively underdeveloped).

In post-Cold War ethnic conflicts (in which we can include the current state of Indian-held Jammu and Kashmir), on the other hand, the descent to partition is accompanied by a widespread delegitimizing of political parties—

through the negotiating process itself—leaving a vacuum which the international community is supposed to fill through its transitional administrations, from 'protectorates' to trusteeships. Historically, though, such administrations have worked only when the countries running the administrations have had a stake in native welfare. The stake generally translates into questions of benefit for the ruling countries, as under colonial and imperial rule. Disinterested international administrations, especially when they are time-bound, run the risks of being hollow at the core, as were the Mandates systems of the inter-war period, which had all the trappings of colonialism without its occasional liberal obligations. But there are also other attendant dangers in the tendency to prescribe international administrations for regions devastated by ethnic conflicts, without seeking to distinguish what is appropriate to which kind of ethnic conflict. This is an especially acute problem when there is a failure to distinguish between decolonization conflicts and new wars. Ironically, the principle of neutralism which informs transitional international administrations, or to put it more accurately. the principle of non-collaboration, applies even where a conflict might fit more appropriately into the decolonization category rather than the new-wars category: in East Timor, for example, a legitimate party is still waiting in the wings almost a year after the humanitarian intervention, despite the fact that it has no challengers, and despite the fact that reconstruction aid might flow more readily if it were in power.

The complex problem of political delegitimization is best observed in Kosovo. Policing—at least in the majority Albanian areas would be much easier if the international administration could make use of the 5,000-strong police force which existed under the parallel government of Ibraham Rugova (a government which was maintained though a decade of repression). But Mr Rugova suffered a personal loss of stature during the Rambouillet negotiations, which also witnessed the emergence of the KLA as a major force. Though the international administration has attempted to bring the two parties together, it has failed to do so. While moves are afoot to transform the KLA into a kind of armed police/security force, civilian policing remains restricted to a woefully small international force, and an internationally constituted academy, which has thus far recruited a few hundred trainees. The Albanian police could, therefore, plug a crucial gap in the areas of their erstwhile authority.

The attached table lays out the best and worst case options which were available during decolonization negotiations at the time of partition, and those which are available in peace processes now. As the table shows, there are a few overarching points to be made.

Peace Processes

First, the conflicts devolved then and devolve now, on contested scales of devolution, from limited autonomy to independence. Ironically, as the table indicates, in many cases, sustained devolution, giving the local people the opportunity to develop democratic institutions, might have worked better than immediate independence (the exit option). This was a point which the international community took on board during the inter-war period, with the Mandates system, which was intended to provide local communities with precisely the opportunities to build institutions which would allow independent states to be ultimately created. (The Mandates did not work in that way, as they were handed over to Britain and France, neither of which, as colonial powers, were well placed to nurture societies to independence. But that is a separate point.) The underlying principle of President Wilson's fourteen points was simply that colonialism was unacceptable, irrespective of its 'civilizing mission': it took a later war, however, to bring the point home.

In a similar way, the post-Cold War period is one in which a new principle is being developed: that sovereignty is not an end which justifies all means. At present, this principle cuts both ways. Intervention against genocide is now an acceptable principle, though what constitutes genocide continues to be debated, and it is obviously par for the course that in the near future this principle will be selectively and rarely acted upon. Meanwhile, if state fiat against self-determination movements is becoming a matter of international rather than merely internal concern, armed self-determination movements/ groups—such as the IRA, the LTTE, and the Kashmir militant groups (which are constantly renaming themselves)—are increasingly seen as impediments to peace in a period in which the international community is relatively more supportive of devolution negotiations than it was either under colonialism or during the Cold War. Indeed, as the history of partition shows, the decision for partition has in every instance been a close call. Not only were alternative proposals for devolution/decolonization proposed, such as the 1945–6 proposal of the Unionist governments in Bengal, Punjab, and Sindh in India for a decentralized federation of secular states, in the majority of cases they represented serious (as against wishful) alternatives, that is they were proposed by parties commanding considerable domestic support, and could, if espoused, have pre-empted prolonged ethnic conflict. Home Rule in 1912, for example, could have yielded Irish Catholic support for the British in World War I: in effect, this would have loosened the tie of guilt and loyalty which the Ulster Unionists used to telling effect with the British government after the war ended, and might have allowed a gradual transfer of power with devolution instead of partition. A similar tale can be told regarding the British in India and in Cyprus: both Indian and Cypriot nationalists would have supported the Allies in World War II had the British been willing to promise self-determination—and this in turn might have paved the way for a phased exit. Indeed, the histories of the five partition conflicts show that ethnic constituencies (and, in a war situation, ethnic territories) consolidate themselves during third party-led negotiations. This consolidation has been generally contested while it was taking place, but the negotiating process itself pushes non-ethnic contestants to the margin.

Yet, as a comparison of the contemporary peace processes in the five cases shows, breakthroughs are often achieved by the marginal rather than dominant parties to the conflict. Arguably, of the five peace processes under survey, the Northern Ireland peace process has been the most successful. Since its inception in the late 1980s, it has progressed by fits and starts, but always incrementally. As a result, though it may appear fragile—to the extent that the executive could be brought down by so minor an issue as the dismantling of a couple of police stations and an army base—its roots are strong. Indeed, the key elements contributing to its success are yardsticks in the other five partition-related conflicts under survey.

(a) A change of heart in the parent nation/diaspora support. The big breakthrough in the conflict over Northern Ireland occurred only when the Irish-American diaspora stopped supporting paramilitary groups operating within Northern Ireland, chiefly due to the spearheading role of the US-based Friends of Ireland amongst the Irish diaspora. This expanded US influence led the British government to start an all-party peace process. Similar hopes have been raised for an acceleration of the Bosnian peace process now that there is a democratic rather than nationalist government in Croatia, though Serbia remains incalculable; and for a settlement in Cyprus, with the cautious rapprochement between Greece and Turkey. In the few months that the Lahore process lasted, there were similar hopes for a Kashmir breakthrough, but these were dashed by escalating hostility between India and Pakistan after the Kargil incursions and the military coup, and remain in abeyance. A change of heart amongst the Sri Lankan Tamil diaspora in Canada and Britain, and possibly more so in the Indian state of Tamil Nadu, could make all the difference to the Sri Lankan partition-related conflict. In contrast, the highly complicated Israeli-Palestinian peace process is frequently confounded by the plethora of contesting, regional, and diaspora supporters.

(b) At the local level, the big breakthroughs are more likely to come from marginal rather than dominant parties. It is worth remembering that at the political level the first visible breakthroughs for the Northern Ireland peace process were achieved by the Social Democratic and Labour Party of John Hume, long regarded as washed up by history. In other words, it is crucial to distinguish between a cease-fire, which only the dominant parties can deliver, and an overarching settlement which will put in place building-blocks for long-term stability. As Britain recognized, for the framework agreements to achieve substance, all parties had to be involved. This is a lesson which has yet to be taken on board by the four other peace processes under survey, though in each of them track-two and track-three are encouraged, to varying degrees. Here is where the differences kick in: in Cyprus, it is possible to conceive of a long-term time-frame, whose first step might be a formal agreement to coexist with the understanding that European Union membership would in time restore freedom of movement of goods, services, and people. Nevertheless, local-level talks will be necessary to work through problems such as the Green Line through Nicosia, the question of property returns and/compensation for refugees, and the fate of Anatolian settlers. Greek Cypriot social-democratic parties and the Turkish Cypriot diaspora could conceivably aid in breakthroughs at this level. From opposite starting points, both India and Pakistan fear all-party talks because of the domestic confrontations such a proposal might entail; yet most people realise that without such talks the spiral of conflict will continue. In Bosnia and Kosovo, where peace rests on still precarious agreements, all-party talks are feared because they might reopen a can of worms. Nevertheless, all-party involvement in social, political, and economic reconstruction is essential if the international community is to have any prospect of an exit. There is an ongoing debate over whether the Madrid talks might not have yielded a firmer Middle-East peace process than the Oslo negotiations did. And while the question might seem academic, it is difficult to see how some of the more complex issues—of refugees, for instance—can be resolved without all-party talks.

(c) A regional framework to underpin peace and move towards long term stability. Membership in the EU played a key role in moving the Irish Republic towards relinquishing claims of sovereignty over Northern Ireland; as Northern Ireland moves toward stabilization under the framework agreements, the EU might now help to dissolve the lines of partition. If the South-East European Stability Pact can be developed, it may be able to play a similar role in former Yugoslavia: however, as it would, by itself, be at best an association of weak states, it would need formal alliance with the EU. In South Asia, there is a crying need for the South Asian Association for Regional Co-operation to be strengthened and its mandate expanded. Cross-border conflicts plague every country in the region, but paradoxically its governments are so deeply suspicious of each other that freedom of movement appears to be available only to militants. Yet these countries are better placed than many others, by reasons of geography, markets, culture, and politics, to form a strong regional alliance. Regional acceptance has been a long-term dream of the Israelis; the problem has been in coming to terms with the Palestinians. Whether and how a regional association can be built, therefore, remains an open but very much present question.

Conclusion

In brief, the overall lessons derived from a comparative analysis of five partition-related conflicts are:

- Partitions do not work as a solution to ethnic conflict. Rather, they restructure the sources of conflict around borders, refugees, and diasporas. Nor, in a post-colonial and globalizing world, do they work either as an exit strategy or as a means of containment.

- While the Dayton Peace Agreement represents an effort to restore to partition its sui generis existence as a separation-of-forces agreement, which could then be a take-off point for a peace process, the lack of strong reintegration policies has meant a downward spiral of partition to ever more, intimate levels. How to turn a partition agreement into a separation-of-forces agreement remains the great challenge for peace-makers, and it may be that we need to turn the question on its head; that is, to look at ways in which a separation-of-forces agreement can be prevented from turning into a partition agreement.

- Here the historical examples of proposed alternative solutions based on a combination of human rights and devolution at various stages of partition-related conflicts, can be useful. Where there is a high level of commitment at international and regional levels, third-party negotiations would do well to draw on the Irish model; where commitment may be partial or weaker, it is all the more necessary to profile alternative proposals.

- When dealing with post-conflict reconstruction, it is important to recognize that the process will be slow unless local communities are involved in both planning and implementation. This point can be further extended to make a distinction between those cases in which potential governments exist, as in East Timor, and those in which putative governments might need to be nursed along. In the former case, the role of an international administration is limited in both time and scope; in the latter, the extent of international commitment needed will vary according to how strong the input into stabilizing the immediate post-conflict phase is.

- Finally, the evolving formula of 'evolution with devolution', in other words of providing a regional underpinning for post-conflict stabilization and peace processes, which has proved so important to the Irish peace process and is being developed with the South-Eastern European Stability Pact, has enormous potential. The fact that the espousal of this formula is still largely limited to the EU should not be a deterrent. Cautious as ASEAN is, and weak as the OAU and SAARC are, long-term stability can be best served by prodding them into growth.

	Ireland	India–Pakistan	Israel–Palestine	Cyprus	Bosnia	Kosovo
Best case option: then	Home Rule in 1912, resulting either in the marginalization of extreme nationalists and unionists, or in a later disintegrative partition war.	Decentralized federation of secular states/unitary state with Jinnah as PM.	UN Partition Plan with economic union/bicommunal, bi-national state.	Unitary state with explicit rejection of Enosis, and full minority-rights protection. Power-sharing through consensual rather than bullying process.	1992. UN/NATO on borders/protectorate Dayton, single army, joint police training; Constituent assembly rather than final constitution.	NATO troops close by during Rambouillet, to prevent ethnic cleansing should talks fail. Demilitarization agreement with KLA after war ended.
Worst case option: then	Continuing civil war, enforced British rule.	Decentralized federation of religious majority states with the likelihood of a later disintegrative partition war.	Unilateral British withdrawal, non-intervention by UN.	Cyprus to Greeks/ *de jure* partition.	Non-intervention, appeasement of Serb and Croat war aims *de jure* partition.	Non-intervention. Mass expulsion of Kosovo Albanians.
Best case option: now	Implementing framework agreements and gradual demilitarization, including phased withdrawal of British troops. IRA participation in decommissioning, restoration of government, police reform. Northern Ireland as part of 'Europe of the Regions'.	Renewal of Lahore process, Pakistan shutting down training and support of mujahedeen/ fidayeen, all-party talks towards autonomy for Kashmir. Settling Siachen, Sir Creek, Wullar barrage disputes, opening trade routes, over time giving substance to SAARC.	Israeli withdrawal from West Bank, Golan and Lebanon, security and water-sharing agreements with Syria, dual citizenship for settlements, right to return Bicommunal, binational state.	Bicommunal, binational state, with countervailing force of European Union membership (freedom of movement, dissipation of partition. Demilitarization. Reintegration of Nicosia.	Substantial investment in South-East European Stability Pact Unified civil service and police training, decommissioning and arrests of war criminals and profiteers, unconditional civil society investment. Return of refugees and displaced.	Demilitarization, decommissioning, border control. Resources for policing, economic reconstruction. Involvement of local communities in planning and implementation of reconstruction.

	Ireland	India–Pakistan	Israel–Palestine	Cyprus	Bosnia	Kosovo
Worst case option: now	Breakdown of police reform, more hitches in decommissioning, continued internal displacement of Protestants.	Indian refusal to talk, Continuation/increase of current 'low intensity' conflict, with ever present threat of wider war, increasing Pakistan crisis, leading to increasing instability spiral from Kashmir into rest of India.	Partition of West Bank, bantustans. Attempt to settle refugee and Jerusalem issues through final status.	Endless proximity talks without results. Unilateral accession of Cyprus to European Union, strengthening, partition, and estranging Turkey from Europe.	Continuing pusillanimity leading to hardening of partition, growing disintegration of state and society.	Spread of cross-border-conflict Partition/propulation transfer between northern Kosovo and southern Serbia. Continuing rise in crime.

DIVIDED COUNTRIES, SEPARATED CITIES

The Last Hurrah that Continues

RANABIR SAMADDAR

Is it not curious, for we all respect the craft of history, that historians writing about independence end up writing about partition; and discussing partition end up writing about messy independence? A history of Partition is a history of how independence came, just as a history of independence relates the impossibility of retaining the dream of independence in its inceptive inno-cence. For Partition is 'contained' within all dimensions of national poli-tics—in territory, citizenship, bureaucracy, group identity, law, literature, language, and now in history. The last hurrah of the Westminster model of de-colonization continues to echo on.

We live in partitioned times; it is within our post-colonial being, in our agony, pessimism, and strivings. One can of course write, when writing of Partition, of its prelude, or of the imperial process of divide and quit, or its residue, or the trauma, the violence, the human sufferings, and the *catharsis*. But this history is lost in the quagmire of the present that does not allow Partition to become a thing of the historical past. Partition's history is thus an incomplete one. At once an event of the past and a sign of the present time, Partition lives on in post-colonial times to such an extent that we should truly prefer the phrase 'partitioned times' to the more common 'post-colonial times'.

The very process of state formation in the 'new areas' of world politics was shaped in a substantive way by the great-power strategy of partition in order to create spheres of influence. Thus was Germany partitioned, and Korea, and then Vietnam, Ireland, India, Yemen, Palestine, Cyprus—all these lands were subjected to partition by the great powers. Radha Kumar's research on

Bosnia[1] has shown how partition has long been a managerial strategy for stabilizing a situation that seems totally out of control, and in the process ushers in a new round of instability. The extent to which the states formed in all these areas in the post-war period have been influenced by that mode of origin has yet to be historically measured and appreciated.

The emergence of modern India came about through one of the largest population transfers in human history. Between 1946 and 1951, nearly nine million Hindus and Sikhs came to India, and about six million Muslims went to Pakistan. Of the said nine million, five million came from what became West Pakistan, and four million from East Pakistan. Immigration into India, particularly eastern and northeast India, has continued under the shadow of the exodus/influx of that time, with new patterns as well as substantive continuities. The impact of crossborder migration on the state and on politics at national, regional, and local levels, in terms of institutionalized and non-institutionalized domains, has been critical but again, unfortunately, inadequately studied. The irony is clear—clearer still when we remember the circumstances of South Asia. The post-colonial nation form was to be the ultimate form of political institution. And the realization of this form—fundamentally through a constitutional process—has required the production of non-state people from time to time. They have been the companions of the entire process of decolonization through wars, partitions, and the deliberate acts of enforcing territoriality.

Modern India today is patently dissatisfied with its origin in 1947: three wars with its neighbour, its own insecurities and insecurity syndrome, the permanent division of the nation into majorities and minorities, the failure of a state-induced capitalist developmental agenda, insubordination of the permanently underprivileged classes, and their refusal to embrace the agenda of the modern nation, all fuel dissatisfaction with the origin. And all this repeatedly 'reopens' the Partition question. As long as the official position maintained that communal violence was madness, Partition appeared as the only rational option; now as genealogical heresy spreads, Partition's legitimacy no longer remains unaffected and can no longer escape scrutiny. Its rationale now appears strictly contingent (thus disputing the inevitability argument); the contingency in turn reactivates memory, creates mythic spaces, and provokes alternative discourses of nationhood. Not unnaturally, therefore, we find the rationalist explanation of Partition being interrogated, reason's externalization—that is, Partition—being investigated by the genealogical heretics.

Partition as a Form of Re-colonization

Thus, what we have to deal with is not an historical event subject to death, but a signed event, an event signed into the present, therefore an event not yet over—not yet even an event. We need to view the representations of pastness as today's political literature, as part of our political being. And that means viewing them as elements in a strategy of political being. This kind of symmetrical convergence of the event with the present requires a different language, capable of producing many commentaries. Reflexive, fabulous, journeying into the origin of the actual event only to zoom back into the present, historicising, and almost at the same time critiquing: the language possessing these attributes has yet to be developed, though its development is in the interest of understanding the fate of such partitioned lands as India. If we can speak of a law of partition, it is that partition not only de-colonizes a land, it re-colonizes it. In short, the law of the existence of partition is its own reproduction through the enforcement of ethnic decrees. The institution of partition attracts the light of nationalism that hides it. The gleam of the instrument hides the sharpness of the effect; the cleanliness of the act hides the un-cleanliness of the result, and the short duration of the enactment does not anticipate its lengthy life span. It took just three months in 1947 for a commission to neatly finish its assignment of boundary redrawing (undivided India). It has taken international political managers and warlords just two years in the last decade to finish off a land (undivided Yugoslavia).

The law of partition thus resides in its method, which enables all symptoms of political convulsions to converge in the irreducible form of partition. This method can be examined in one of two ways: either by showing the difference between earlier acts of separation and dismemberment—the non-national and the pre-national imperial forms—and the decolonizing, re-colonizing forms of today; or by showing how today's politics cannot exist other than in partitioned times. Our theoretical instruments must go beyond the tired debates around continuity and discontinuity and really grasp the nature of the method that has made our politics what it is today.

Partition leaves independence in its wake, a dream of sovereignty fulfilled; as such, it is combined with optimism. At the same time, it ensures only partial fulfilment of dreams: it spreads dejection and pessimism; it creates the impossible desire for pre-partition days and pre-partition lands. It realizes the dream of a homeland, but at the price of creating what Salman Rushdie calls 'imaginary homelands'.[2] All kinds of footloose people emerge at the end of the tunnel—refugees, migrants, immigrants, vagabond widows, exiles, and aliens who will forever live in these imaginary homelands. Never happy to transact their identity of escapees of violence with a certification of citizenship, they impart a continuous instability on the state born out of partition, and to the state-system engendered by such de-colonized, re-colonized states. In this 'pessoptimism', to use Edward Said's well-known neologism, there is all pervasive excess. In grief and hope, remembrance and amnesia, quarrelling and the gesticulations of making up, this excess is to be seen. Repetition and excess become ways of spiritual life for the nation and all the other political communities aspiring for nationhood. Partitions create not only imaginary homelands; they create ethnic decrees to pursue those homelands; they unleash memories that become the sites of fascist politics.

Invariably such memories are fragmentary. Memory becomes the passion of the mind, and victimhood becomes the soul of the nation. Everyone becomes a victim of the victim. The nation is the victim of the imperial policy of divide and quit. The minority becomes the victim of the nation. Individual refugees seeking shelter in the other half of the partitioned land become the victims of the alien state that they had considered their own, and which they now discover to be their unwilling host—for the state, too, claims to be the victim of conspiracies. In this excess, partition becomes a tempting tool for a final solution of the footloose situation, of the inherent and impossible tensions that accompany the political history of migration, displacement, democracy, and self-determination. It is not enough to point out that partition leaves in its wake powerful memories that no history can explain or anticipate. We require, if we are to understand the politics of that memory, an understanding that can cut through the ambiguity of de-colonization, appositely expressed in an even more ambiguous term, post-coloniality. Contrary to commonly held belief, modernity is in dire need of memorial exercises, simply because the modern is the most hegemonic way of exercising power, and so does not rest until memory too is colonized. With memory at the service of state formation and state consolidation, the passage of time can smooth out wrinkles. Memory's truth defeats the political truths of the time. Partition creates 'pessoptimists' who are good subjects for literature, photographs, poignant plays and films, but singularly incapable of re-democratising the politics of the land. In this milieu of a sleepwalking nation, where instability is the sign of the times, the only stable institution appears to be in the form of a cartographic act that will solidify all that was melting into air. The act of redrawing the boundaries is therefore only the beginning; its life—or larger-than-life—begins thereafter.

Ethnocracy and Pseudo-homelands

Thus does partition create majoritarian states, which one may refer to as ethnocracies?[3] In this development, five factors merit our attention: the irreversibility of the time of partition; the specific character of the violence through which partition was brought about; the substitution of the logic of majority for that of plurality; the geopolitical imagination lodging itself at the heart of postcolonial politics; and finally, the mystery around the history of partition—the problem of the knowable and unknowable.

Let me begin with the issue of the geopolitical imagination of the nation, essential for it to turn into an ethnocracy. Lying before us, beyond the intellectual arguments about the required history of the birth of a nation, we see the partitioned region of South Asia, de-colonized and arranged into a system of states. It will not be irrelevant to remind us here, that globalization is itself mediated through the order ushered in by partition. Out of what used to be only Hindustan, or simply the subcontinent whose margins vanished imperceptibly into another region—the Turco-Persian part of the continent—Partition created South Asia. The undefinability of its borders is gone forever, the home where the nation was born is now lost and a region that has been constructed on the reality of vivisection now yields a variety of homelands, symbolizing a home that is gone and is able to relive only in the form of reflexive images; more accurately, in the form of reflexive nationalisms, which are we all know as homelands.

Now that Partition and the succeeding fifty-three years have ruled out any easy or programmatic resolution of either complete reunification or total dispersion, the implication is one of both universality and difference, for the many values of old pre-Partition times were never enough to ensure mutual respect. Europe is increasingly talking of reunion. Southeast Asia is talking of union in the form of association. People are learning from them and want South Asia to 'return to its history and geography like one returning home'. But returning where? To a common cultural space? But culture would mean, first of all, identity—that is, difference with others, and then difference with (in) itself. How then to accommodate the differences, the permanent process of creating 'others'? Or return to a common economic space! In truth, marked by multiple colonial linkages and the exclusion of the majority from the 'economy', there never really was a common economic space at all; this common economic space can arguably be created, but cannot be returned to. Return to a common historic space! But this historic space includes partition, and thus we cannot return to it while excluding that epoch from that space. Like every history, this history of partition—that is, the history that created it and the history it created—can be summarized. How, then, can we include this summary in this other history of commonness, whose summary will comprise other movement, other memory, promise, and identity! All this simply means we cannot return, but only turn on an acknowledgement of differences: the differences of a unity, in unity, with another unity.

We have still other reasons to inquire into the way partition has marked the creation of the region called South Asia. This process of a region coming into being has interestingly been accompanied by the rediscovery of old fault-lines. Orthodox and fanatic Islam, backward sub-regions, non-patriotic frontier tribes, small neighbours prone to blackmailing the stable and strong nation, historic connections with other regions, natural areas of influence: all these are being rediscovered, much in the same way fault-lines are being rediscovered in Eastern Europe in the process of region-making in Europe today.[4] The irony, in short, is this: in the region-making of South Asia, unity is the theme—that is how the nation is to return home. But in forging a policy of uniting, it rediscovers the old fault-lines—in fact, the nation has to redefine and mark them out in order to erect the new political-economic and security arrangements on which to relate. Therefore, designations of underdevelopment, permanent fundamentalist threats to liberal values and civilized existence, backwardness, and so on, become the reinforcing material for a neo-modernization theory which can map out the cultural region of South Asia—the home of the nation. That is how the core of the region is built. In the resultant marginality of certain elements required to build a regional core, Partition remains the reference point.

Thus we have not one, but two declarations of independence and decolonization, which we celebrate in recalling the birth of the nation. One celebrates the advent of the independence of nations, the rise of South Asia as a distinct region, the beginning of decolonization. The other announces the advent of a fractured region, the validation and legalization of the conservative approach to community empowerment, and the strategic success of a policy of weakening the left. It announces the creation of a milieu allowing strong residues of colonial ways of power, and finally the strengthening of the rhetoric of a 'besieged fortress' that justifies a call by the new right to support traditional values and cultural homogeneity. The later has sancti-fied a political scene where the issue of collective representation has been usurped by the reactionary demagogues who have now acquired legitimacy and a clear advantage. The result is a strict policing of the community's mores, a paranoid suspicion of other groups—the easiest way to create a sense of national and/or communitarian unity. In short, this Janus-faced independence gave South Asia political power, democracy, and an assurance that the dream of ethnic liberation was worth pursuing. It also created both communities of the afflicted and aliens in their own homeland.

How, then, is the persistence of the naive belief that 1947 was not a Janus-faced event—that it only created two (subsequently three) independent states—to be explained? That, although the vivisection may have been unfortunate, accommodation between the states will undo the contradictory aspects? If, as seems clear, minority categories (religion, language, territory, tribe) in this region, called the 'home of the nation', are historically formed and continuously in the process of formation, then there cannot be any easy recourse to an administrative or state-centric solution, assuming that such categories are fixed points of descriptive reference. In making such categories absolute, there is a populist substitution whereby what they are 'today' replaces the more complex accounts of their historical location, differential access, and internal cleavages. The breakdown of such categories as entities therefore always seems both sudden and ridden with eternally un-learnable experiences, whereas the analysis of the institutional operation of the parti-tioning categories remains unsatisfactory.

More important in this context is the strength that the psychological framework of the populist right has gained from the politics of combining identity with territory. Partition provided an abiding lesson to the populist right: namely, that identity politics are not necessarily a threat to conserva-tive goals and constituencies. The co-optation of identity politics by the populist right since 1947 has presented the Left with three major problems: (i) conservative constituencies have proved well-suited for a 'cultural war' in which different communities fight for their mutually exclusive empower-ment; (ii) their success has stemmed from the fact that a populist mixture of reactionary ideology and anti-establishment feelings have been undeniably empowering in the sense that a community's empowerment has become synonymous with the increase of its leaders' prestige and power; and (iii) in the long run, liberals have been pushed to the right. This new right, basing itself on populism, has achieved success because its programme is moralist: it is a loosely organized movement, strongly anti-intellectual, opposed to the 'establishment', and ultimately communal, nationalist, often xenophobic. Again, this success was clearly demonstrated in the agenda and act of Partition and has capitalized on that experience.

It would be wrong, however, to equate Partition with the rise of the populist right in the postcolonial politics of South Asia. At a more funda-mental level, the birth of our nation raises the question of modern represen-tative politics in the post-colonial conditions of South Asia. The representative political system is based on the representation of necessity, identity, and the self—in other words, of interest. Where interest has mostly been articulated around a group or collective, the representational problematic has to do with organizing hierarchies of representations. On the one hand, representational politics validates the nation, which is the highest group or community; on the other hand, it has to give space to other interests, hierarchically—for by according supremacy to the nation, it has admitted the logic of hierarchy. Therefore, the genealogy of the citizen in South Asia is caught in the representational bind. If citizenship in South Asia has thus been a transac-tional identity only—based on the necessity of exchange of unequally en-dowed individuals, and of unequal agencies—it should not cause surprise, for the language of citizenship in South Asia has been embedded in collectives of various kinds for too long to be discarded by any liberal rhetoric about the clean birth of the nation.

Peter Miller has written that 'the history of thinking about citizenship, like that about the state, belongs to the vast category of things ancient made modern by their adaptation first by Christians and then by medieval Italian urbanites—the difference being that when we use "state", we intend the modern definition, whereas when we use "citizen", we intend the ancient, anachronism notwithstanding'.[5] Partition was the instrumentalist solution to these dilemmas of hierarchy, anachronism, and necessity, because it was thought that by partitioning the polity (and, hence, the society) the problematic of representation would achieve the most drastic, and most modern, solution—though as can be seen now, the problem remains at the heart of the solution. Partition has exposed the nation to the deep instability latent in the notion of representation and citizenship. Globalization has not minimized the instabilities; by accentuating the particularities of both self and the communities, it has accentuated them. Salman Rushdie has com-mented that writing of one's homeland from abroad is like being obliged to deal in broken mirrors, some of whose fragments have been irretrievably lost. Though he may not know it, the experience is similar for those who never left.

Of course, in spite of being battered from within, where all problems faced by the nation seem to have both internal and external links, the nation must have a place under the sun, if not necessarily 'a place in the shade'. Buffeted by the simultaneous process of rapid globalization and massive regionalism in various parts of the globe, the nation in India finds itself in a world that is unfamiliar and deeply disturbing. The political parties also realise their limited influence in this process of region making, as they had been working since Partition almost solely under national laws and paradigms. Economic dissatisfaction and political alienation have led to autonomy movements or movements based on local identity. The local is now being redefined, and new regionalizing links—mistakenly called 'sub-regional links'—are being rediscovered. In this milieu, the notion of territory is assuming increasing importance. Again we can mark the hour of Partition as the beginning of a territorial consciousness.

Up into the fifties and into the sixties, the leaders of this nation had ambitions of having a place under the sun—the glory of an independent nation had not yet rusted away. But world events, the decline and ultimate collapse of the Soviet Union, the increasing irrelevance of the non-aligned movement, the crisis of a bureaucratic-capitalist economy, and the increasing realization that the area of South Asia could not be made into an Indian 'national lake', all brought the limits of a South-Asian power into the open. The ambitious actor's role remained cruelly unfulfilled. Ironically, the realization of the impossibility of being a world player led to the alternative—that is, of being a major power in Asia, the hegemon of the region, which in effect has meant sometimes being the green helmet of the peace-keeping or punitive forces in distant lands.

Almost three hundred years ago, Montesquieu pointed out the difference between kingdoms and republics: namely, that kingdoms want to achieve glory through international action, whereas republics pursue long-term interests. But parliamentary regimes and today's republics in many cases follow the policy of the kingdoms of olden days. George Bush wanted America to recover from defeatism and regain self-esteem through the Gulf war. In South Asia, too, glory has become the objective of the republics. Territorialism has become an essential part of the policy to attain glory and this territorial consciousness, we can say, almost begins with Partition. Inevitably, therefore, a foreign policy based on territorialism and aimed at glory, prestige, and healing national frustrations, has brought back to surface the very differences in the historic heritages that had begot these same frustrations and had resulted in territorial losses and shrinkage fifty years ago. The political project of a South-Asian unity is therefore impossible, unless the problem of territorialism is solved democratically, or through the conquering sword of the major power. The current impossibility of disentanglement of the territorial problem prevents the nation from embarking upon 'grand politics'—the type of policies which attract the imagination of the masses and provide glory, standing, and rank. Acknowledgement of this inadequacy to engage in grand politics has led to trying for the second best—if not a place under the sun, at least for a place in the shade.

There is always a danger in seeking this place however. For it means ignoring the past of Partition and the unclean birth. We are faced with the banalization of our past—the past of Partition—and a desire to develop our 'own' geopolitics, ignoring that it was the event itself that first led to this search.[6] The geopolitical imagination that lay at the heart of Partition has led to a theology of the border. Borders convey sanctity; yet born of Partition, and therefore negotiated daily by thousands of people, they are now naturalized. Just as borders are the product of Partition, the mental borders conjured up by the geopolitical imagination of the nation-in-the-making gave birth to partition as well. In this connection one has to only read the meticulously researched essay by Joya Chatterjee on boundary delimitation and demarcation in Eastern India by the Radcliffe Commission.[7] It leaves no doubt as to the explosive result of a combination of geopolitical imagination, territorial politics, and nationalist democracy. The geopolitical ambitions and imaginations linger and increase; they numb our revulsion at a rogue past.

It is necessary, therefore, to understand the issue of territorialism as the product of Partition in a more concrete way. By cutting the territory, and making the task of guarding the territory (as defined by the colonial rulers as India: we have to only think of the British frontier policy in the sub-continent) an imperative, Partition has accentuated territorial consciousness in the region. The logic of territory, namely standardization, formalization, centralization, and configuration (euphemistically known in the region as 'territorial integrity'), has now turned into a state-strategy for rationalizing and exerting influence and control. Originating in an 'unclean partition', the territorial consciousness of the nation in the sub-continent will eternally disturb the neatly segmented universe of the standard political map of this region. For the result of 1947 was not only a partition of territory, but also the foundation of a new system of states in the region—one that is prone to be revised again and again. The superimposing maps of dreamland states drawn by Rehmat Ali, now hung in the Lahore Museum, speak of the strength of the geopolitical imagination active in the subcontinents. What is surprising therefore, is not the uniqueness of Rehmat Ali's imagination, but the extraordinary similarity of the spirit of those maps with the inherent instability of the geopolitical imagination of the nation in South Asia.

Ethnic Space and the Irreversibility of Time

Space plays, therefore, a crucial role in the emergence of majoritarian states. Yet we need to bear in mind while discussing this emergence of ethnic space the extreme significance of the sense of the irreversibility of time. Because Partition appears as the final act—perhaps undesirable but unavoidable, perhaps bloody but necessary to avert more bloodshed, perhaps an unhappy separation but a separation to prevent genocide—the irreversibility of partition overwhelms the nation, its leaders and public. In this situation, the public mind becomes an ethnic mind, for the nationalist public discovers itself in the comic form of identity, which can only assume an ethnic form. To the extent that democracy becomes a victim of the nationalist strategy to use Partition to achieve statehood, ethnicity wins out. Partition inverts the relationship between nationalism and ethnicity on the one hand and democracy on the other. It is the irreversibility of the act that makes this inversion possible.

After sacrificing democracy and embracing partition, what form can the nation take other than ethnic? When democracy proves insufficient for providing a collective name, when anti-colonialism and anti-imperialism prove similarly inadequate, and a democratic resolution of the 'question of the nation within the nation' proves impossible, it is time for the irreversible final step towards statehood. Yet, and this is the strangest part, no one takes this step, it just presents itself, and everyone bows to the inevitable. Thus, you have the run of assertions: the British did not divide the country; they had no alternative but to bow to the wishes of the subjects. The Muslim League did not cause it; it was forced to seek a homeland due to the Hindu Congress's obduracy in sharing power with the Muslims. The Congress did not want it; but to avoid genocide, it was forced to accept a divided India. Partition appears as the axe of God, and the nation must go forward to attain statehood. Time is therefore as important as space in giving birth to the post-

colonial politics of state and nation. Ironically, only the decolonized understand how ethnic space builds on ethnic time.

Besides building on the irreversibility of time, the ethnicization of the
nation takes place through the irreversible seizure of the nation by patriarchal political power. The non-democratic aspects of a nationalist politics
that had wanted to negate at every opportunity the independence of various
political formations now reach their apogee. The, sacrifice by the state of
countless women to implement partition and secure the post-colonial order
represented the final assault of a nation that was fast turning into an ethnic
formation.

Surprisingly again, excepting a handful of unrepentant left intellectuals,
few historians have connected the violence against women and the violence
against the peasants. Of the countless books on Partition, we have few works
on violence against women, and fewer still on violence against the peasants.
Fortunately, studies by Urvashi Butalia, Ritu Menon, Kamala Bhasin,[9] and
others have attracted some attention, though lamentably, they are still read
as feminist histories and not the history of a counter-revolution. But studies
such as Amalendu Sen Gupta's *Uttal Challish—Asamapta Biplob* (The surge
of the forties—the incomplete revolution) are lost. In the discourse of
Partition, no one refers to the almost simultaneous peasant uprising. That is
another history, a vernacular history, pushed out of centralized narrative.
Amalendu Sen Gupta has written in Bengali, others have written in Hindi,
Assamese, Telegu, still others in Malayalam and Urdu; however, in the
centralizing narrative of Partition and state-formation, those histories are
lost. Quarantining the deviants such as the women, the rebellious peasants,
the obdurate political sects, the indigenous peoples, Partition was implemented and the post-colonial state was formed. Built on the irreversibility of
the decline of all other fortunes excepting that of ethnic destiny, the nation
marched into statehood.[10] A cursory look into the deliberations of the Indian
Constituent Assembly is all that is needed to see how the nation went back
on the promise of a new deal for minorities, on accords with various unwilling
political formations, how it became one of the key instruments of passive
revolution. So severe was the discipline effected by nationalist violence on
society—and so complete was the hegemony—that historians long needed
(social) sanction to narrate the other story of independence.

Existing accounts of independence thus became the prison guards of
other accounts. Framing a history to silence certain voices: what, exactly, is
meant by this in the context of our effort to understand the secret hour of the

nation's birth? The history of the Partition of India remains incomplete without the narrative of how this history is built upon silencing counter-voices. The rise of the various radical movements since 1942 is well known. There is now enough documentation on the activist and rebellious mood of the masses and on the radical mass upsurges during 1945–50. It is curious that those who should have been most proud of this legacy and of the fact that it characterized the times of Partition are, in fact, embarrassed by it and hesitate to accept them as the counter-voices to the process of decolonization through Partition. And those who speak of the specific experiences of the people during the Partition era do not speak of the experiences of their uprisings, their defeat at the hands of the state, the colonial power and the forces soon to assume power. And, expectedly, those obsessed with the search for a history of secularism versus communalism (including the defeat of the former) do not link these events at all; they are an embarrassment to all. It is, however, worthwhile remembering that this exclusionary framing and pre-mature narrative closure were inevitable in the process of Partition and decolonization itself—in short, in the genesis of the nation.

When Dreams Dry Up

The silence about the complexities of Partition, about the extraordinary coincidence of the radical upsurges, and the transformation of the radical mood of the Muslim masses into communal activism, about the 'peasant utopia', suggests the premature closure by the social and disciplinary forces of the political and ideological establishment, by information management and an ensuing collective self-censorship. In East Bengal it was said: 'What Tebhaga?[11] Why fight for it? With Tebhaga you get only a share, with Pakistan you get the whole.' We shall require a great amount of research into the discourse of Partition in all the three countries—India, Pakistan, and Bangladesh—to come to a full understanding of the silencing process. Without it, the birth of this nation remains a theoretically knowable but actually unknown history, which makes the consideration of the various versions of the event part of the history of the event itself.

What happens when dreams dry up? I shall suggest four consequences and quickly go through them in order to suggest that Partition's principal func-tion is disciplinary. While historians are busy looking at the dark side of the independence of the new nation—namely, violence, homelessness, and hatred as the cardinal principle of politics—let us draw ourselves away from the narratives of insanity and see what they mean in terms of democratic politics. First, constitutionalism (whether or not it succeeds) in the new nations naturalizes the dark side, and, promising a return to normalcy, marginalizes the dissenters and heretics. Second, this normalcy, based on an act of violence and hatred, kills the spirit of reconciliation. The polity can then speak only of retributive justice and not restorative justice. The promised restoration of dignity after the hour of retribution never arrives. Third, democracy becomes organic—in other words, intolerant—and the people so defined by democracy refuse to accommodate other peoples, not so defined by democracy, and push the latter out.[12] And finally, the issue of self-determination, which caused the political managers so many sleepless nights, resolves its own dilemmas by a bizarre technique. It kills all others selves to such an extent that there need not be any other self but only the geopolitical self of the aspirant. Several essays would be needed to work out the history by which the modern state arrives; Tilly calls it contentious history. But we can say this much: that a theory of the passive revolution, which inevitably accompanies state-formation, must investigate these aspects to find out why Partition has become the universal act in the age of liberal democracy, and why Partition has become the institutionalized form of our domestic and geopolitical histories.

Notes

1. Radha Kumar, *Divide and Fall? Bosnia in the Annals of Partition* (London: Verso, 1997); *See* also the review essay by Arvind N. Das, *The End of Geography*, Biblio, March–April. 1998, pp. 8–9; on this theme further, Clive J. Christie, 'Partition, Separatism and National Identity—A Reassessment', *Political Quarterly*. 63 (1), January–March 1992, pp. 68–72.

2. Salman Rushdie, *Imaginary Homelands: Essays and Criticism, 1981–91* (London: Granta Books, 1992), pp. 9–21.

3. I am indebted for this term to Oren Yiftachel who uses the concept in his essay. 'Ethnocracy and Its Discontents' Minorities, Protest and the Israeli Polity', *Critical Inquiry* 26(4), Summer 2000.

4. The best instance of such rediscovery is of course S.P. Huntington, 'The Clash of Civilizations?', *Foreign Affairs*, 723, 1993, pp. 22–49; Huntington, 'If Not Civilizations, What? Paradigms of the Post Cold War World', *Foreign Affairs*, 725, 1993, pp. 186–94. On an analysis of such paradigms in regionalizing Europe, Elizabeth H. Prodromou, 'Paradigms, Power and Identity: Rediscovering Orthodoxy and

Regionalizing Europe', *European Journal of Political Research*, 302, September 1996, pp. 125–54.

5. Peter N. Miller, 'Citizenship and Culture in Early Modern Europe', *Journal of the History of Ideas*, 57(4), 1997, p. 728.

6. Even perceptive observers miss the role of 1947 in the development of Indian geopolitical thinking—an event that marked the shift of the nation from marking out a cultural region/area to a geopolitical area as its 'natural habitat'. *See*, for example, a RAND study by George K. Tanham, *Indian Strategic Thought—An Interpretative Essay* (Santa Monica, CA: National Defense Research Institute, 1992).

7. Joya Chatterjee, 'The Fashioning of a Frontier—The Radcliffe Line and Bengal's Border Landscape, 1947–52', *Modern Asian Studies*, 33 (1), 1999.

8. These maps are of 'Pakistan in 1757', 'Pakistan in 1847', Pakistan, Dravidstan, Bangastan, Uttarstan, and so on.

9. Urvashi Butalia, *The Other Side of Silence—Voices from the Partition of India* (New Delhi: Viking, 1998); Ritu Menon and Kamla Bhasin, *Borders & Boundaries—Women in India's Partition* (New Brunswick, N.J: Rutgers University Press, 1998).

10. See the admirable survey of ethnic cleansing by Andrew Bell-Fialkoff, *Ethnic Cleansing* (New York: St. Martin's Griffin, 1999), particularly Chapter 3, 'Cleansing as a Metonym of Collective Identity', pp. 57–115.

11. Tebhaga was the agrarian struggle in Bengal in 1946–9, the name deriving from the sharecroppers' demand for a rightful share of the produce.

12. Michael Mann, 'The Dark Side of Democracy—The Modern Tradition of Ethnic and Political Cleansing', *New Left Review*, 235, May–June 1999.

History as Drama*

FRIEDRICH DIECKMANN

It is often overlooked that the German Democratic Republic was not only a country with extensive dramatic production, but itself constituted a work of art that complied with the rules of classical drama. Ascending and descending action, climax, tragic element—it is all there, strictly in keeping with Gustav Freytag,[1] and it could be turned without much effort into a presentable five-act drama, a piece that would satisfy all the requirements of art, including the fact that the turning points of the ascending action already contain the finale, the final point of the descending action.

The Experience of Revolution

17 June 1953 and 13 August 1961 are such turning and nodal points, both of them excellently suited as act endings. The 17th of June 1953 marked the end of the second attempt by the Soviet Union to get rid of the GDR which they had been forced to set up without wanting to. One year earlier, in March 1952, Stalin had made the first attempt, which had been better prepared. The second attempt, abruptly decreed by Beria and put into action incompetently (or sabotaged with perfection) by Semionov,[2] led to the overthrow of the powerful Minister of the Interior by a coalition of his opponents; between these two events there lay that bleak period which, in July 1952, was given the name 'Creation of the basis of socialism'. That year alone, between the summer of '52 and the summer of '53, could stand on its own as an outstanding German drama.

* Translated from the German by Esther Kinsky

The 17th of June brought Act One of the GDR to an end. A conceivable final scene: in the Central Committee building the invited guests toast Hermann Matern, the most powerful man in the party after Walter Ulbricht, on the occasion of his sixtieth birthday, while the windows of the entrance hall are shattered under the pressure of the demonstrating crowd. There is general consternation. Zaisser, the former Spanish Civil War general and Beria's underling, turns pale, Mielke sighs with relief: he and Ulbricht are saved. Beria's plan to give up the GDR has been thwarted by the attacks of the demonstrators: the Russians have to intervene, the GDR continues to exist. But, as befits a well-structured drama, the focal point of the ascending action contains the finale *in nuce*: the spectre of a repetition of the 17th of June, the fear of violent incidents which would have deprived the Soviet leaders of the fruit of their policy of détente, initiated with such effort and difficulty (they would have had to intervene again, and all the confidence in their country which Gorbachev and Shevardnadze had been able to build up would have gone down the drain), were the reasons why the country was given up in the course of the autumn and winter 1989, after forty years of hanging onto it. The GDR, an abandoned work. In 1994 that is the name B.K. Tragelehn gave his play about the aporias of production, a play that was three quarters finished in 1962 when he put it in some remote drawer in his study from where he retrieved it thirty years later. History itself had given it an ending.[3]

Act Two

1953–61, with an interlude in 1956, when the Hungarian uprising in November and its bloody suppression by the Soviet army stabilized Ulbricht's reign once more, although it had never actually been under serious threat. It is this very fact—no prospect of Ulbricht's dismissal—which, in the late summer of 1956, the Soviet ambassador Pushkin tries to explain (in a significant scene) in a four-hour conversation with a malcontent who is fiery and obtuse in equal measure. The name of the malcontent is Wolfgang Harich, and he is rather slow on the uptake: he stubbornly tries to convince the Soviet representative that Ulbricht's dismissal would serve the interests of the Soviet Union, as it would pave the way for a rapprochement between the SED and the SPD and ultimately help create the peace-loving united Germany the Soviet Union has so unwaveringly called for. The philosopher playing the politician has no idea that Khrushchev triumphed over Beria in

1953 mainly because the army leadership would not tolerate the surrender of the GDR as planned by Beria: for the army, the East German state was the pledge and bastion of their victory over Hitler's Germany. In 1956, unlike after Stalin's death, Ulbricht's position was not seriously threatened, so the time between Khrushchev's party congress and the suppression of the Hungarian uprising was no more than an—admittedly suspenseful—interlude in Act Two of the drama of the GDR, leading up to a spectacular final scene: the closure of the border in 1961. This, too, represents a turning point in the ascending action: deflecting the crisis, it already contains the play's finale. When the SED leadership announced the opening of the borders in November 1989, the state, which had closed itself off so tightly, soon met its demise.

Act Three

1962–71: the ascending action reaches its climax which marks the turning point. Again, dramatic interludes intervene, for example in 1965, when the policies of reform, introduced in many sectors in the GDR two years after the erection of the wall, are thwarted by the Moscow leadership: the Brezhnev era makes itself felt. The chief economic planner[4] reaches for his service pistol when he is asked to sign draconian treaties, a steam roller levels the hopefully sprouting cultural terrain. Act Three, too, is made of stern stuff. Three years later, a heightened, variant version of the story is enacted in a neighbouring country, which the Russians eventually invade. In the GDR, they had been present all along.

But there too, 1968 is a volatile year: on the one hand, microelectronics is given a big push forward, on the other there is the demolition of churches and a new constitution. The party monarch, by now the undisputed ruler, wants to force technical-industrial progress and simultaneously cement autocracy, and in the pursuit of this aim he occasionally displays the same degree of vandalism as Mao's dreadful wife at about the same time. VEB Robotron at the same time as the blowing up of the Pauliner Church in Leipzig: progress + regression from ONE source, each in excess. But neither one is real, and the combination of both even less so. The author of these actions can claim one more victory, but it is the last time.

Thus Act Three, too, is full of dramatic events: the echo of the shots at the Ussuri[5] river reverberate in its final scenes, after that everything changes in Europe. In the 1971 finale of the act, the ascending and the descending action converge, this is the double climax. The general diplomatic recognition of the GDR—worldwide and by its German brother country—is imminent; at the same time, the autocrat is overthrown by his henchmen. The finale is memorable: one evening in April 1971, almost the entire SED leadership arrives at the Soviet embassy to be sworn in for the overthrow of their leader.

Act Four

In Act four, 1971–81, the descending action takes its course and there is no shortage of contrasting elements. The state reaps the fruit of the policy of détente: UN membership, more than a hundred diplomatic missions, a secretary of state as the accredited representative of the West German chancellor. But, at the same time, momentous diversions are becoming rampant: the leader of the youth movement,[6] promoted to leader of the pack, declares—with a stage-worthy mix of subservience, greed, and fear—class war on the remnants of private economic property which have long since been integrated; while restrictive cultural policies become more relaxed, micro-electronic investment is pulped. Cheese not computers is the new motto, and, to the delight of the entire population, the cheese involved is of French origin. In other words: progress + regression the other way round, and again with the aim of keeping a balance. A fantastic intermezzo: the expatriation of the singing Bolshevik;[7] conspirational intermezzo: five top ranking politbureaucrats attempt to persuade Brezhnev by letter to help them dismiss their commander who is all too keen on running up debts in the west. The sombre final scene of the act: the price of oil is falling, a cause for grave concern, because the country has got used to selling Soviet oil at maximum profit for 'valuta', the magic word of the new era meaning western currency. To the east of the Oder and Neisse, the Polish army defeats a Catholic workers movement to the west of these rivers, adolescent pacifists are hunted down, they wear the words: 'Swords into Ploughshares' sewn on their clothes.

Act Five

The fifth, and final act, covers the years 1982 to 1989, and, as in Frank Castorfs theatre productions, it is marked by a gradual expiry of the plot. At the beginning, there's Brezhnev's funeral with wheels of flowers in flaming red behind a carriage flanked by members of the Guards' battalion in mournful goosestep. A Berlin interlude: the dismissal of a would-be pretender to the throne called Naumann,[8] anticipated by a slim book with the title *Hinze-Kunze-Roman* (Tom-Dick-Harry-novel).[9] The artist of the people dictates the tribune's departure, this is new, developments are beginning to change colour. As the change in colour in Moscow becomes perceptible, the protagonists become increasingly paralyzed; and in the end—no, we can dispense with the description of this finale, we remember it well enough. The play, as we see, is structured in astonishing conformity with the rules, with the action fading out—an original element—and a grand tableau for the finale: the object of history, known as the people, declares itself the subject and surrenders itself to new leaders of objects of unbroken vigour and infectious optimism.

Arrival

It sometimes happens that fellow Germans in the West assure a citizen of the former GDR that he or she has 'arrived in the Federal Republic'. These incidents always remind me of the story of a woman from the GDR who, on the occasion of a family visit to the West—which had become much easier in the eighties—spent an evening with the friends of friends over a glass of wine. Having heard where the visitor was from, they asked her in a polite conversational tone: 'Is this your first time in Germany?' This happened to more than one person, and there were two possible reactions. Either one broke out in tears or laughed out loud. The former is entirely understandable, but I've always preferred the latter.

Klaus Schlesinger[10] has a sequel to this story, it is told as a joke, but there may be a real dialogue behind it. It is presented as a dinner conversation between two Hamburg businessmen in 1991. One of them says to the other with some amazement: 'It's only been two years since the collapse of the GDR, and already everything is in German hands!'

'What is German?'—Richard Wagner's question, posed in 1865 in anticipation (and disapproval) of a German-German war, seems to remain unresolved.

Have I arrived in the Federal Republic? Yes, and not just since today. As resident of the new federal Land of Berlin, I arrived on 3 October 1990—along with seventy-million German citizens, and almost seven million residents of other nationalities—in this state which had been re-established as 'united Germany' by the peace treaty, signed on 12 September of that year in Moscow by the four victorious powers of the World War II and both German

States. It had never been dissolved, and I had always lived in it, and consciously so: it is the state which was founded in 1866 under the name of the Norddeutscher Bund (North-German Federation), following the above mentioned German–German war, also known as the Prussian–German war. The state whose citizen I became, together with sixteen million residents of the GDR and over sixty million residents of the former Federal republic, was that state revived, but at the same time it was an essentially new one. Its reinstatement was, unlike Bismarck's foundation, not the result of a German–German war but the—by no means painless—decision to avoid and avert a war of this kind. At the root of its revival there were no wars but an event in which peace and freedom had but *one* face: the opening of the concrete border in Berlin.

It was like a miracle but it didn't come out of the blue; it was a miracle facilitated by many very different people on both sides of a border that was considered impervious to softening up. The road that led to it, from a situation marked by universally accepted stagnation, has already been forgotten by many who weren't living close to it at the time. It may sometimes seem as if 1990 saw the reintegration of a renegade province and not the unification of two German states of which one, in the East, had in a process, first of reform, then of revolution gained the popular sovereignty which its trustees had previously allocated themselves as if by the mercy of God. For the population of West Germany which emerged even from World War II without any changes in socio-economic power relations, revolutions are the epitome of the inconceivable. A society which within one generation, and with an interval of only forty years, has even experienced two revolutionary caesurae, first the radical change of economic power relations after the demise of the Hitler regime and then the fall of the politbureaucratic power apparatus at the peak of the Gorbachev era (both historic changes occurring under the same occupying power), a population like this is inevitably enigmatic to them, unless knowledge, interest, and sensibility have created quite different presumptions.

Revolutions, the use of force to establish a new state of law in the place of an old one that has failed, are neither beautiful nor good, but they constitute historical facts. By virtue of these facts, the population of the part of Germany which in 1945 fell to the occupying power that had made greater sacrifices in Hitler's war than any other nation or state, became linked to a history of revolutions which began, albeit unsuccessfully, in the Germany of the peasant wars, continued in seventeenth century England, spread to

France in the eighteenth century, and after World War I transformed Russia. The internal and external link to five centuries of revolutionary experience constitutes the particular path within German history which led to the foundation, existence, and dissolution of the German Democratic Republic. It was not by coincidence that a Frankenhausen panorama became its largest, and also its most significant, painting. Unveiled in 1989, the gigantic circular painting became the epitaph of the state that had commissioned it. The painter[11] had painted his country to the end.

The conscious link with a European history of revolution, itself originating in Germany, is a societal factor which, seen from the German West, can be comprehended only rationally, if at all. The same thing applies the other way round: from the viewpoint of the GDR, it is equally difficult to appreciate a society which has survived the disasters of the century with its property structure and the resulting power relations intact and seeks to atone for this surprising fact (the existence of the GDR was its reflex) by generating continuous feelings of guilt. The problem of these mutually exclusive experiences is unresolved, perhaps beyond resolution, and therefore a source of continuous misinterpretation and misunderstanding. It is obvious that the latter are repeatedly instrumentalized. and then they are vivid reminders of the way the SED used to invent a reality favourable to its requirements of power, and, dependent on the individual case, borrowed a semblance of facts for it.

Ligatures

In the German democratic revolution, it was the working class, which was not only *pro forma* the ruling class in the GDR (its loss of power was one of the most significant consequences of the changes) which refused obedience en masse to the state. It was workers who wrecked Dresden's main railway station in violent clashes with the police on 4 October 1989, when trains with refugees from Prague were passing through. By taking flight to the west in the summer and autumn of 1989, young working-class families unwittingly drew the conclusion that the overall privileges for the working class (which went hand in hand with discrimination against white-collar workers and the intelligentsia) had clogged up the very source of technical progress which in other places was a fantastic stimulus to the supply of commodities. This progress had undermined the technological foundation on which the existence of the working-class had rested for over a century and subsequently provided the basis for the growth of the working-class movement. In the socialist states, where those in power had seen themselves from the beginning as the political ruling committee of the industrial proletariat, the fundamental micro-electronic revolution destroyed plebeian absolutism from the outside just as, in the eighteenth and nineteenth century, the industrial revolution had destroyed the absolutism of the feudal class from the inside. This plebeian absolutism was as far removed from the Nazis' murderous mob regime as from the pluralism of western consumer societies; its hierarchic-centralist way of functioning corresponded to the factory structures which constituted the elementary socio-economic experience of the workers.

At this point, it seems advisable to make something of a digression. The form of society which classified itself as developed socialism to indicate (and deceive itself) that it had lost its original dynamic—the gigantic dynamic of the social melting process—and undergone a gradual, pseudocristalline consolidation, could be defined as a structure which, as a result of the systematic demotion of the money and profit factor in economic activity, lowered the temperature of the society to such an extent that it fell below the melting point of social liquefaction and that its increasing viscosity resulted in a cristalline appearance which gave the congealed liquid the semblance of a solid body.[12] The demotion of the profit principle sought to overcome the process of the capitalization of all social relations—as described by Marx with visionary intensity—by withdrawing it; and this was in fact the crucial cul de sac and fundamental paradox of the monopoly socialist structure of society.

In the course of this withdrawal, specific binding forces had to be brought into play after the completion of the social melting process; the model for this was the hierarchically structured factory collective which constituted, as noted above, the basic social experience of the majority of Communist officials. This production collective was fundamentally different from the collective of frontline soldiers which had become the centre and seed of the fascist organization of society. The difference between the Communist and the Fascist system, including the difference in its stability, is largely the result of the difference between these two models of cohesion: the producing collective and the destroying collective.

The leadership situation was also different. The factory collective is led by the foreman or chargehand. a man who belongs to the same class as his subordinates. The collective of frontline soldiers is led by the aristocratic or bourgeois officer who in the face of death—and only in the face of death— becomes an equal among equals. Both collectives. the producing variety and the destroying variety. are the contrasting manifestations of an epoch—the industrial epoch in the phase of electrification and the chemical industry. The industrial worker at his workbench and the infantry soldier at his machine gun are ONE subject, allocated opposing roles by one and the same system; breaking away from its spell while either one of these forms of experience establishes itself as dominant proved an illusion—each in its own way and yet in diametrical fashion.

The Communist and the Fascist organization of society both have their roots in the view from below; they are grounded in the contrary-identical basic experience of trench and assembly line. This experience organizes itself in opposition to those heights of society where the bourgeois factory owner looks at the stock-exchange reports and the aristocratic field marshal at the battle plan. That the revolutionary consciousness determined by the collective of frontline soldiers was able to join forces with these two figures from the heights against the rule of the proletarian production collective is related to the mode of its formation and to its inherent destructiveness alike.

The factory collective as the hierarchically structured production family belonging to ONE class determined in the transpositional form of the party group the entire power and economic apparatus of the monopoly socialist state. Just as the competition of parliamentary parties appears as the reflection and counterpart of the competition of free-market entrepreneurs, the rule of the party group spanning all organizations from the cell up to the politbureau is the counterpart of that factory collective which had itself been created by the entrepreneur competing on the free market. The entire state, including its economy, functioned like the production process of ONE factory: monopoly capitalism in the strict sense, but without entrepreneurs and to a certain extent without capital, because the relationship between different enterprises, determined by the need for market dominance and profit, was precisely what was outside proletarian experience. As the factory collective had taken shape historically only as a result of free enterprise, the political generalization of this collective could entertain the belief that it constituted a more mature social formation. Marx's idea of the free association of producing individuals had overlooked the fact that after the elimination of the entrepreneur the only social experience left would be the workers' collective moulded by the entrepreneur and a particular level of technology. As their product, it could have no interest in a change of the mode of production.

Exposure

In the late phase of Honecker's rule, the state concentrated the effectiveness of the binding agents, produced by the basic moulding of factory collective and party group, in the concept of 'shelteredness' as opposed to the 'exposure' of the molecule of bourgeois society. Some Western observers are meanwhile inclined to equate this shelteredness with outside pressure and enforced enclosure, simply for the sake of the expectation that as soon as the barriers have fallen, the exposed individual will joyfully leap onto the new stage of freedom. But the border regime and other security apparatuses were only the external condition of a society which would never have been able to exist, if it had not developed specific forms of social cohesion under the conditions of isolation.

The mirrored inner wall of a thermos flask is the condition of the ice inside not melting. But it owes its existence as ice not to the wall but to molecular cohesion: the insulation only prevents it from melting. It may be psychologically plausible to associate this cohesion with a greater degree of warmth, as is sometimes suggested metaphoricallly, it is nevertheless misleading insofar as it is precisely the insulation from warmth, from the higher temperature of other kinds of social processes that preserves this molecular package in its imitation of a solid body while in reality it is merely in a particularly viscous state.

At the economic and the social level, state socialism was defeated by the computer—a development Walter Ulbricht tried to overcome in the late sixties when he embarked on an impossible mission: to establish the GDR as the pioneering country in the field of micro-electronics. A system which had undertaken to organize the whole of society on the basis of the old industrial worker's sense of work, had to founder not only on the costs but also on the nature of the new instruments of production. The old machinery had created a particular form of cohesion among those who were subordinated to it in their work. This bonding which crystallized at the political level in the shape of the party group had been the elementary particle of monopoly socialist society. It could not outlast the micro-electronic revolution.

One way of binding the individual to his or her workplace was the wide range of social and cultural facilities attached to it, which contributed to the fact that the work collective, whether at the assembly line or in the office, assumed the characteristics of an extended family. It functioned as a second family for those who were not 'employees' (*Arbeitnehmer*) but 'work operative'

(*Werktätiger*), these newly coined words, the flat, bureaucratic one as well as the freemason-like elevated one, reveal the difference in conditions. The factory which was not an enterprise (its managers were in fact civil servants) was called an operation (*Betrieb*), operated by work operatives who did not receive work but gave it, and many perceived it as the primary level of a quasi familial experience for the good reason that people spent much more time in the work-place family than in the domestic family. The social control of the individual through the density of this clanlike collective bond was the strongest and most fundamental of all control mechanisms of the monopoly-socialist society—a supervision which, as in a real family, was closely bound up with care and assistance.

The security apparatus of Mielke's ministry, which, out of a sense of political helplessness, but also in keeping with the internal law of multiplication of bureaucratic populations, grew out of all proportion, was the parody and perversion of this basic social condition in which the plant management and SED-group were the authorities which visibly exercised power, followed at some distance by the trade-union group which allocated bonuses and vacation places. The uncommon interest which the secret voyeurism of the Stasi-apparatus aroused in the public voyeurism of the free media corresponded to this *tertium comparationis* which in both cases assigned itself a moral weight—one at the level of state morality, the other at the level of individual morality. The ludicrously inflated apparatus of the Ministry of Security revealed itself as an extreme case of a total apparatus whose problems originated in the very aporias of progress. Relating its industrial-technological demands to forces of cohesion rather than dissolution, namely with the intention of encouraging them, was an undertaking no less paradoxical than wanting to use a refrigerator as a cooker. And it worked accordingly: external and internal pressure, border regime, and doubly and, triply secured administrative integration enforced a closeness of the social molecules which was simply not suited to the increasingly heated nature of the production process. It became obvious early on that the notion of promoting industrial progress without increasing the kinetic energy of society was an illusion: pointing to the symptoms of this insoluble problem is only of cognitive value if one has previously understood the profound paradox of the phenomenon. But the fear of advancing from the surface of the symptoms to the core of the contradiction manifests itself everywhere and often bears neurotic traits; it certainly doesn't follow the course of former lines of demarcation.

This fear is related to the pressing urgency and topicality of the problem on whose antinomies socialism-turned-state unconsciously wore itself out. It is obvious that one cannot overcome a blindly self-perpetuating progressive development by moving back to a state that predates this process; one cannot reduce the temperature of a global process by artificially withdrawing warmth or forcibly keeping warmth away from it. It even seems impossible to just keep the temperature from rising. After two centuries of an industrial melting process, global society has once again drastically accelerated the energy of its particles through new technologies; if the temperature continues to rise it will inevitably undergo a change of its state of matter which will not necessarily occur abruptly, gradual transitions from liquid to gaseous state are familiar from nature.

This image from physics does not only apply at the metaphorical level. At a strictly physical level, the mobility of the individual in the highly developed countries performs the transformation of the potential energy stored within the earth and matter as coal, oil, or nuclear energy into the kinetic energy of a social molecule which, by virtue of technologically domesticated fire, is auto-mobile in all other elementary spheres: on land, on water, and in the air.[13]

This physical mobility, whose real costs are hardly registered in any budget, combines with the kinetics of that weightless information mobility which increasingly dominates production and leisure. While Gutenberg's mobile letters were the initial invention of bourgeois society, the microelectronic processor appears to be the thermal seed of the post-bourgeois state of matter. Its thermic efficiency corresponds to the weakening of the binding forces which tied the people of former ages with more scarce available energy supplies to their social, intellectual, and topographical place.

The problem of asylum seekers is only the outer surface of a condition defined by the thermal pressure of global lead and top temperature on traditional societies and would not exist without the global-mobility effect of television, airplanes, and the internet. It is of a symptomatic nature, just like those safety nets of state socialist orders which, entangled with themselves and the totality, function in a social condition of artificially reduced heat as peculiar refrigerating machines. Restricting one's gaze to isolated phenomena is as predictable as it is evasive: it prevents a society, which no longer has an unsuccessful pseudo-alternative at hand to stabilize itself, but is now mercilessly confronted with itself, with its own contradictions, so painfully revealed by new demands, from comprehending its own situation. Approaching boiling point, it reassures itself by looking back at the abstrusities of the attempt to outdo production society by lowering the temperature of communications processes. It finds it difficult to understand that, in its very failure, this attempt regained the urgency which already marked its beginning.

Notes

1. Gustav Freytag (1816–95) well-known novelist, author of *Soll und Haben* and *Die Ahnen*, who also wrote a theory of drama *Die Technik des Dromas* (1863) and a play *Die Journalisten* (1854),

2. Vladimir Semionov (1911–92), Soviet politician, senior responsibility for foreign policy and an expert on Germany, active between 1945 and 1953 in the Soviet-occupied Zone (as ambassador and High Commissioner of the USSR in the GDR). Beria saw in him the instigator of the uprising on 17 June 1953 in the GDR, designed to thwart the German plans (Reunification on the basis of bourgeois democracy) entertained by the chief of Security who was aiming to become Stalin's successor. The uprising contributed significantly to Beria's fall on 26 June 1953. *See* S. Semionov, *Von Stalin bis Gorbatschow* (Berlin, 1995), pp. 290 ff.

3. See 'Neue Deutsche Literatur', NDL Heft 495, 1994/3 History itself has written it.

4. Erich Apel (1917–65) President of the State Planning Commission and Deputy Prime Minister.

5. The lower and middle reaches of the Ussuri River mark the border between China and Russia (i.e., the Soviet Union). In 1969, there were serious clashes between Soviet and Chinese troops along the border, triggered by the occupation of an island in the river. The threat of a Chinese-Soviet war was a significant contributing factor in the ensuing policy of détente pursued by the Soviets in Central Europe.

6. Honecker who was the president of the youth organisation (FDJ) in the Soviet occupied zone or GDR.

7. Wolf Biermann who gave himself that title.

8. Konrad Naumann (1928–92) was head of the SED in Berlin and a member of the Politbureau of the SED until 1985. His successor was the journalist Günter Schabowski.

9. By Volker Braun.

10. Klaus Schlesinger (1937–) well known GDR author who left for West Germany in 1980. Recent publications: *Von der Schwierigkeit, Westler zu werden*, Essay (Berlin: Aufbau Verlog, 1998); and *Trug*, novel (Berlin: Aufbau Verlag, 1999).

11. Werner Tübke (1929–) leading member of the group of painters in the GDR

that became known as the 'Leipzig School'. His panoramic painting in Frankenhausen (Harz) illustrates the peasant wars and the Reformation. It was in Frankenhausen that Thomas Münzer fought his last battle at the head of the rebellious peasants in 1526.

12. See Friedrich Dieckmann, *Temperatursprung* (Frankfurt: Suhrkamp, 1995).

13. Friedrich Dieckmann, 'Der apokalyptische Punkt oder Zwei Wege zum Sonnenstaat', *Merkur*, no. 582/583, September 1997.

The Partition of India[*]

CLAUDE MARKOVITS

The twentieth century saw the partition of at least four great empires. The First World War brought with it the partition of the Austro-Hungarian and Ottoman empires, along with the First partition of the Russian empire, subsequently reconstituted as the Soviet Union, before it was itself swept away by the winds of history at the end of the twentieth century. In each of these three cases, partition was the direct consequence of a military defeat and the political transformations to which it led. However, it is the partition of the Indian empire in 1947 between India and Pakistan which is some-times attributed the status of a paradigmatic event, no doubt because it came about not as the result of a world-wide conflict, but instead somewhat arbitrarily divided up (in a time of peace) a political entity to which its rulers ascribed a certain homogeneity, and was accompanied by inter-community violence and massive displacements of population. The recent partition of Yugoslavia, marked by massacres and forced migrations, seems to provide a confirmation of this paradigmatic status. Less attention is paid to the fact that the partition of the former Soviet Union, like that of former Czechoslo-vakia, were generally speaking violence free (with the exception of the conflict between Armenia and Azerbaijan). The following paper is some-thing of a reaction against the dominant view which ascribes paradigmatic status to the case of India, seeking to restore its full specificity to the painful event, before envisaging the more general lesson which may be drawn from it.

---

[*] Translated from the French by Stephen Wright

The Historical Context

Pakistani historians generally begin their accounts of Pakistan's birth with the evocation of the Great Mutiny of 1857, better known as the Sepoy Mutiny. This reference to an anti-British uprising, in which Muslim elements played an important—though not predominant—role enables these historians to set Pakistan squarely in the continuity of a history of anti-imperialist struggle and to take the opposite point of view from their Indian colleagues—for whom the Partition resulted above all from the machinations of British imperialism in its phase of decline. Beyond these ideological differences, which are of course not unimportant, serious academic Partition history—a discipline born in the 1960s, both in India and Pakistan—traces back the origins of Partition of the 1930s, at which time a specifically Muslim sensibility began, with Jinnah's influence, to assert itself within the nationalist movement. The Muslim League, an old organization of notables, created in 1904 to counterbalance the Indian National Congress, which certain members of the Muslim elite considered overly dominated by Hindu circles, began its transformation, under the leadership of the future Qaid-e-Azam (great leader)—himself a supremely anglicized Bombay lawyer —into a mass political party at the very time when, in 1937, the Congress for the first time, within the framework of political reform, attained governmental responsibilities at the provincial level. For a brief moment, it seemed that Muslims' aspirations to have their specificity recognized were not incompatible with the creation of a united independent India, but from 1940 on, the paths of the Congress and the League separated definitively. Whereas the former chose the route of new confrontation with the British, the latter, for the first time at its Lahore session in 1940, came out in favour of the creation of a separate political entity for the Muslims of India to be known as Pakistan—whose shape, moreover, remained fuzzy. The process through which this vague project ended up leading to a territorial partition between two distinct sovereign states in August 1947, remains the object of divergent interpretations.[1] Until the mid 1980s, most of the credit (or responsibility) was given to Jinnah, but Pakistani historian Ayesha Jalal's[2] iconoclastic biography, published in 1985, threw many certainties into question. Some people have emphasized the role of the Congress leaders, Nehru and Patel, who, in spite of Gandhi's opposition to the very idea of partition, preferred a clear-cut decision and were prepared to accept a truncated India rather than power sharing with Jinnah and the Muslim League. But we are not so much concerned here with explaining the event as with evaluating its meaning and impact. The consequences, however, can still be very directly felt more than fifty years after the fact, for a serious dispute arose in 1947 between the two new states, centred above all around the Kashmir—that has only grown over the course of the past five decades—and which, after having led to three conventional wars, threatens to trigger at any moment a nuclear conflict in the heart of Asia. The Partition of India in 1947 gave rise to a new territorial reality, without however essentially changing the populations' relationship to the territories. Thus, in the minds of the actors themselves, Partition remains, at various levels, unfinished. It is a tragedy, whose fifth act has not yet been played, and for which catharsis has not yet come about.

State, Territory, Nationality in South Asia before and after Partition

Nowhere was it written that South Asia would not evolve toward the edification of relatively homogeneous national states. During the medieval period, a process of ethnogenesis—in many ways comparable to the one Europe went through, and to which the flourishing of vernacular literatures bears witness—was at work, and could have provided an impetus for such a development. The creation of Muslim empires from the twelfth century on, first in the Delhi Sultanate then, following an Afghan interlude, the so-called Mogul empire—created by the TurcoMongol descendants of Timur, the Timurids—led the subcontinent in another direction. The downfall of the Mogul empire beginning in 1730, meant, however, a resurgence of regional states, some of which, including the Mysore and the Maratha Confederation, turned out to be fairly durable constructions. The British conquest then brutally interrupted the process of political recomposition that the subcontinent was undergoing. The empire which the British set up in India between 1757 and 1858 was an original political construction. It offered a particular place for certain elements of the indigenous elites. Thus, up until 1947, a quarter of the Indian population lived in princely states of various shapes and sizes but in which they found themselves subjected to Indian princes, who governed, like absolute monarchs, under the more or less distant watch of British representatives, as subjects deprived of political rights. What came about in India in 1947-8 was therefore not only the partition of a unified whole, but also the reunification of these princely states with British India. That is a point which is all too often overlooked. The threequarters of the population living in the India subjected since 1858 to the direct domination of the British crown (after having experienced that of the British East India Company between 1765 or 1818 and 1858), found themselves in the paradoxical situation of being full-fledged subjects of the crown (entitled to the protection of His Majesty's consuls when travelling abroad) without however being entitled to any political rights until 1909. A series of political reforms in 1909, 1919, and 1935 progressively attributed Indians certain rights, but not that of designating those who governed them who continued to be envoys from London, utterly foreign to the country. These reforms were not granted by London through sheer kindness of heart, but represented gradual and partial concessions to an opinion ever more influenced by nationalist ideas.

The conception of the nation which was developed from 1870 on by the ideologues of Indian nationalism, oscillated between a purely territorial definition (all inhabitants living in a geographical area defined by 'natural borders') in the tradition of French nationalism, and a definition making allowance for ethnic and linguistic criteria in the style of German national-ism. Ethnicity in the Indian context was defined above all on the basis of religious criteria, for the linguistic situation was particularly complex, and did not contribute in any significant fashion to defining differentiated groups. The question of identity and belonging arose mainly with regard to the Muslims, the principal religious minority, unequally spread out over the territory, in a polity dominated by Hindus (though there were also other religious communities in India). The principal leaders of the Congress, and in particular Gandhi and Nehru, were relatively sympathetic to the 'territorial' definition, in which Muslims were included in the Indian nation; minority elements, however, amongst whom the ideologue of Hindu nationalism, Savarkar, gave their preference to a combination of factors that were both territorial (India's holy land) and cultural (belonging to a Hindu culture, designated by the term Hindutva), which tended to exclude Muslims. The latter—or at any rate, members of the Muslim elite—long hesitated between loyalty to the British, pan-Islamism, or prudent adhesion to nascent Indian nationalism. From the 1930s on, Jinnah and the leadership of the Muslim League promoted an essentially cultural definition of nationality. Jinnah put forth the idea that there were two distinct nations in India—a Hindu and a Muslim nation—characterized by different cultures (rather than by differ-ences of a religious nature, for Jinnah himself was not a practising Muslim). Transforming this cultural nationalism into a territorial nationalism was not self-evident, because the religious communities lived in a fairly intermingled fashion over the entire Indian territory. The areas in which there was a Muslim majority were 'peripheral' regions (Punjab, Sindh, Baluchistan, North-west Frontier Province, East Bengal), where most of the community was made up of peasants of often very unorthodox practices, influenced both by Hinduism and Sufism. The Muslim League was weak in these areas before 1946: its essential base was in the regions in Northern India, which had formed the heartland of the former Mogul empire, and where most of the elites and historical sites of Indian Islam were located. The territorial division which occurred in 1947 between India and Pakistan took no account of these cultural factors: it was inspired by demographic logic alone, which was itself the product of colonial census-taking. Overall, the regions with a demographic Muslim majority ended up attached to Pakistan (with the exception of the Kashmir valley, which was part of a princely state whose maharajah was Hindu, and chose, in 1947, under very particular circum-stances, to join India), and the regions with a Hindu or Sikh majority were incorporated into India. But, one way or the other, no consultation of the populations themselves was undertaken (except amongst the population of the Northwest Frontier Province, who chose, by a slim majority, to join Pakistan). When the division came about on 15 August 1947 (the actual borderlines—which had been drawn up by a commission chaired by a British judge who knew nothing whatsoever about the context, Sir Cyril Radcliff—were actually only announced two days later), there were millions of Hindus and Sikhs on the Pakistani side and tens of millions of Muslims on the Indian side of the border. No population exchange, of the sort Turkey and Greece had carried out in 1923, had been envisaged during the complex negotia-tions which preceded the partition. Yet, though neither of the two states, even Pakistan—in spite of the two-nations theory—had claimed its adher-ence to a 'community-based' definition of nationality, and even as their leaders were multiplying reassuring declarations and appeals to the popula-tions to remain where they were, the facts spoke for themselves: on both sides of the border, in particular in the Punjab, millions of members of the 'minorities' sought to flee to the other side. In the Punjab alone, which had slightly more than thirty million inhabitants, ten million people thus passed from one state to the other in 1947–8. These massive displacements were accompanied by largescale massacres, whose death toll is generally evaluated at a half a million. Faced with this situation, the two states were obliged to accept the fait accompli, and beginning in September, in order to avoid total chaos, they took charge of organizing and protecting the convoys of refugees, which led immediately to the decrease, and later the end, of the violence. Regarding the kidnappings of women which had systematically occurred during the massacres, a doctrine of nationality came to be elaborated, which was based upon belonging to a given religious community. It was decided of common accord that the kidnapped women had to be returned to their community of origin, even if they preferred to remain with their family of adoption and had converted to the religion of their kidnappers (which, in fact, may sometimes have been their protectors, men who had married them to save them from rape and dishonour). Any Muslim woman discovered on the Indian side of the border in a Hindu or Sikh family to which she did not belong through birth, was ipso facto declared to be 'Pakistani' and sent back to her family of origin (who often did not want to take her back, considering her forever dishonoured), and the same fate awaited the Hindu and Sikh women discovered in Muslim families in Pakistan. Overall, 30,000 women were 'recuperated', 22,000 Muslim women in India and 8000 Hindu and Sikh women in Pakistan in an operation which only came to an end in 1954, but which could not heal the physical and moral wounds inflicted upon tens of thousands of women on both sides of the new border.

The tragic events which went along with the partition of India reveal the conflicting coexistence in the subcontinent of two different conceptions with regard to territory and nationality: one which makes residency the essential criteria of nationality, and the other which gives priority to considerations of community belonging. Once the worst of the crisis was over, the territorial conception took over again, above all in India where Muslims represent more than 10 per cent of the total population (and 90 per cent in the Kashmir valley) and are considered officially as full-fledged citizens, enjoying the same political and civil rights, even if in fact, they are particularly hard hit by certain types of socio-economic discrimination (which moreover vary from one region to another). But even in Pakistan Hindus remained (less than 2 per cent of the population), who also enjoy civil and political rights. Nevertheless, counter tendencies are at work which threaten the minorities' positions: in India, a government based upon the ideology of Hindutva exerts a certain amount of pressure—fairly discreet for political reasons—on Muslims in order to favour a cultural 'homogenisation', which could translate into measures of a legislative nature, such as the adoption of a uniform civil code (for the time being, each religious community has its own family code), while in Pakistan, an incessant process of Islamization threatens to make the lives of the Hindu, Christian, and Ahmadi minorities more difficult.

The Human Legacy of Partition

Above and beyond the massacres and terrible physical and psychic pain suffered by many of the survivors, some of whom were never able to get back to the 'normal' course of their lives, the major legacy of Partition was the identity-based rift which came about in the lives of millions of individuals suddenly torn from their familiar frame of life, their lands (the majority of displaced persons were peasants), and their ancestral homes in the name of an utterly abstract principle: the principle of nationality which had only limited significance for them—even if in fact it was based on affiliation with a religious community. The latter, however, was far from totally defining the field of identity in India. Thus clan and caste-based affiliation, often so crucial to the definition of social identity, did not always correspond to religious divisions. In the Punjab, the large peasant caste of the Jats was made up at once of Hindus, Sikhs, and Muslims, and certain Jat clans had members belonging to the three religions. The division even affected certain extended families. Yet all the emotional and material ties which had been woven in the course of the centuries between various segments of society across the religious divide were erased in the paroxysm of the situation: in the Punjab in 1947, each individual was perceived either as Muslim, Hindu or Sikh (the latter two communities being largely united in the confrontation with the Muslims, even if they had areas of contention amongst themselves, which were to crop up in India several years later). The polarisation stemming from such a situation did often not make it any easier for the mass of Punjabi peasants—whether Muslim, Hindu or Sikh, who had to move from one part of the province to the other to integrate the event into their usual mental categories. Yet they did adapt, and after several years of hardship, on both sides of the border, rebuilt their lives and often showed a dynamism and a spirit of enterprise which was superior to that of their compatriots of local origin. This adaptation was facilitated by the linguistic and cultural community which existed in both parts of the Punjab (in spite of the existence of regional variants).

Paradoxically, the transition was more difficult for the displaced who belonged to the lower-middle class, who left from other provinces. in particular for the Urdu-speaking Muslims from Northern India, who emigrated in considerable numbers to Karachi and Sindh, where they were known as Muhajirs; and for the Hindus from East Bengal who, from 1950 on, increasingly poured into Calcutta and other cities of the Indian West Bengal. These mostly urban refugees left, generally speaking, of their own will, in a context characterized by a fairly limited level of violence. The Muslims from Northern India, in particular those from the cities of Uttar Pradesh, had, prior to 1947, been the most fervent partisans of the Muslim League and of the movement for Pakistan, and the decision to emigrate that some of them made was often inspired by an idealistic enthusiasm for the new state. They abandoned possessions and homes and generally left apart of their family in India. But when they got to Sindh, they discovered a local Muslim population that was culturally very different and which greeted them without great enthusiasm.[3] They did not mix with the local population and created sorts of enclaves in the principal cities, above all in Karachi, where they fairly soon constituted the majority of the population. They remained nostalgic for their cities of origin and faithful to Urdu, which they made into Pakistan's official language. During the first decade of Pakistani history, they occupied a dominant position in the new state's administration and political life, but at the end of the 1950s, their position underwent a certain erosion with regard to the ascension of a military-bureaucratic class recruited in the Punjab. In the course of the 1960s and 70s, they developed a minority syndrome and at the end of the 1970s had turned into a genuinely new ethnic group, with its own political party, the MQM (Muhajir Qaumi Movement), which relied upon them to claim a major role in the political life of Karachi and Sindh.

The trajectory of the Hindu refugees from East Bengal was very different. Belonging generally to the urban lower-middle class, they left East Pakistan more progressively, from 1950 on, driven more by considerations of economic opportunity than by political allegiance. When they reached West Bengal, they found an urban milieu where their social category was already over-represented and thus had a great deal of difficulty making a place for themselves—despite the linguistic and cultural affinities with the local population. Some became proletarianized, and formed the principal base of the Indian Communist Party in Calcutta in the 1950s; others managed to set up shops and small businesses which struggled along. Their particular identity was above all manifested through such attitudes as their support for one of the big football clubs in Calcutta (where the model, imported from Great Britain, of social and ethnic polarization around two or three big clubs came about in the 1950s), but they never experienced any long-lasting 'ethnic' crystallization, and, from the 1960s on, merged with the mass of the Hindu population of Bengal. Even the new influx of refugees linked to the Bangladesh crisis in 1971 was not able to curtail this trajectory of assimilation—though it did not rule out a culture of nostalgia.[4]

It can thus be seen that the refugees of the Partition dealt with their situation in various ways. The great majority fairly quickly integrated into the life of the country to which they had come by force or by choice. There remained in Pakistan the question of the Muhajirs, that community of several million people from the north of India and their descendants, who formed a veritable ethnic group, politically organized, and in a state of partial dissidence with regard to the official Pakistan.

However, although the majority of the refugees were fairly successful in terms of their integration, the memory of the event itself, on both sides of the border, remains traumatic. Phenomena can be observed which recall those of the memory of another traumatic event: the Shoah. Initially, indeed, a heavy silence prevailed, broken only by several literary works, from such authors as Sadat Hassan Manto in Pakistan and Khushwant Singh in India[5] and whose immediate impact was in any case fairly limited. The violence that went with Partition was largely concealed in public discourse, and its memory remains confined to the realm of private pain. As I showed in another text,[6] the historiography of the Partition which was put together in the 1960s and 1970s was above all of a political nature—and very 'elitist'. It was interested in the 'high politics' of the Partition and tended to exclude the question of mass violence to focus above all on the calculations and actions of the main actors, such as Jinnah, Gandhi, Nehru, and Mountbatten. However, since the end of the 1980s and the early 1990s, there has been a spectacular 'return of the repressed'. The resurgence of violence between Hindus and Muslims in India in the 1980s—which culminated in the destruction of the Ayodhia Mosque by Hindu fanatics in 1992, and which in Pakistan led to retaliations in the form of the destruction of numerous Hindu temples—brought the question of violence back to the fore, and showed just how easily emotions could still be stirred. At the same time, the new interest of feminist historians for the question of the kidnapped women[7] brought attention to this painful and previously neglected aspect of the events of 1947–8. Suddenly, more studies and testimonies were coming out, above all on the Indian side, and a new historiography opened up which sought to place the mass of anonymous actors—both the perpetrators and the victims of the violence—at the core of its preoccupations. The question of the relationship between memory and history was raised in a way that recalled certain European lines of questioning around the Holocaust.

It is nonetheless important to emphasise the differences between the two events. They are comparable neither in terms of the extent of the massacres nor above all in terms of the type of violence. The subcontinent in 1947–8 bore witness to no organized state-driven extermination, making use of the full gamut of available modern techniques of control and organization; but rather to an array of techniques which combined the 'modern' (the use of military methods often acquired during the Second World War by numerous veterans, both Muslim and Sikh, who flanked the mobs of rioters on both sides) and the 'traditional' (the use of rape to humiliate the adversary, the mutilation of 'enemy' bodies) in the service of limited objectives which were of a 'communitarian' rather than state-driven nature, such as 'ethnic cleansing' of a territory to expel the members of the other community. A detailed analysis of the systematic attacks on trains which took place in the Punjab in August 1947,[8] in which the majority of the victims of the massacres perished, makes it possible to pinpoint this mixture of modern and traditional aspects. These attacks were, in general, carried out by small bands organised in military fashion and supervised by veterans or deserters from the army with expertise in methods of sabotage and the derailing of trains. They acted generally speaking on information received, and did not attack the trains blindly. Nevertheless, the way in which they perpetrated the massacres, often with a knife and carrying out mutilations, referred back to a more traditional universe. In this respect, one cannot but be struck by a certain resemblance between the massacres which accompanied the Partition of India and those which steeped the former Yugoslavia in blood between 1991 and 1995. And yet, there too, it is important to be attentive to differences. The various acts of 'ethnic cleansing' carried out in the former Yugoslavia generally followed plans which had been drawn up in advance and that corresponded to precise political objectives, of a 'state-driven' nature. The point was to achieve a recomposition of the ethnic landscape, by creating a certain number of ethnically homogeneous entities instead of a situation where different ethnic groups were fairly mixed. In the case of India, things were far less clear. Of course the Punjab was cleansed of its minorities: the Pakistani Western Punjab became almost exclusively Muslim (with the exception of a Christian minority), and the Indian Eastern Punjab became utterly Hindu–Sikh (also with a Christian minority). But there is no evidence that this 'cleansing' was truly premeditated on one side or the other. It was rather the product of a multitude of local initiatives, triggered by an infernal cycle of reprisals and counter-reprisals fed by the constant circulation of rumours, which, in a largely illiterate society, played a considerable role. These local initiatives benefited from the passive or active complicity of members of the administration, police, and army—all of these institutions being themselves affected by the atmosphere of inter-community hatred which prevailed at the time. The only genuine 'plan' seems to have been that of the Akalis—the Sikh 'fundamentalists' and their leader, Master Tara Singh—who sought to regroup the bulk of the Sikhs in a part of the Punjab in the hope of being able, at some future date, to claim an independent Sikh state (a claim which was indeed expressed in the 1980s). In the India and Pakistan of 1947–8, 'communitarian' logic and state-driven logic were combined to a certain extent but not totally coterminous, and it is this point which constitutes a difference with regard to the events of 1991–5 in the Balkans. For, in the chain which links communitarian and state-based logic, territory constitutes an essential link. In India, however, as social anthropologists have long since pointed out, territoriality is rarely a central aspect of groups' identities—or was not, at any rate, prior to the contemporary period. There existed a certain flexibility in this regard. Thus in 1947, the majority of the Sikh leaders supported—more or less under duress of course—a partition plan, which placed some of their holy sites on the Pakistani side of the border. For upholding the identity of the Sikh community did not depend on the political control of a given territory.

In the case of India, it is useful for methodological purposes to separate the analysis of Partition as a pan-Indian political event having its roots in the recent political history of the subcontinent from the analysis of the massacres themselves, a paroxystic event lasting only a very short while (a few weeks) concerning above all the Punjab, the explanation of which cannot avoid taking account of the whole region's militarization linked to the Second World War (it was the Punjab which provided most of the Indian troops who fought on the various fronts from Malaya to Eritrea and Italy). In fact the massacres were not the inevitable consequence of the partition: one can imagine that Partition could have come about without the same level of violence if all of the actors had been aware of the dangers of the situation and if in the Punjab there had not been the unfortunate coincidence between particularly strong inter-community tensions, fuelled by certain decisions (such as the definitive drawing of the borderlines, which deprived the Sikhs of some of the holy sites which they had hoped to hold on to) and the presence of competent military supervision and an abundance of weapons.

It would thus be hazardous to draw overly general conclusions from the case of India on a necessary correlation between the partition of multiethnic political entities and the outburst of inter-community violence. In the same way, it would be erroneous to see in the creation of Pakistan the confirmation of the impossibility for Muslims to live in a political entity dominated by non-Muslims: after all, despite the 1947 Partition, some one-hundred and twenty million Muslims live in India as a minority which, though often threatened, has by and large been able to hold on to its individuality. And it should be pointed out that their common belonging to Islam did not prevent the Muslims of western and eastern Pakistan from tearing each other apart and finally splitting in 1971 at the cost of another partition, which gave birth to Bangladesh.

The Partition of India in 1947 remains in the history of the twentieth century a *sui generis* event, the result of political tensions linked to the unequal penetration of democratic ideas in a society which was culturally and socially extremely heterogeneous, rather than the resurgence of centuries-old hatreds, as is sometimes imagined. The extent of the massacres, which went far beyond not only the 'normal' level of violence between antagonistic communities, but even the exceptional level which was seen since 1946, can largely be explained by the militarization of the Punjabi society—itself reinforced by the massive recruitment carried out during the Second World War. The Partition of India, whose roots reach back to the 1930s, and whose direct and indirect effects can still be felt today, represents an historical episode of a particular duration and complexity. To confer upon it paradigm status in the framework of a comparative study of partitions therefore strikes me as a hazardous venture at the methodological level.

Notes

1. For an account of these events and an attempt to interpret them. I refer the reader to C. Markovits (ed.). *Histoire de l'Inde moderne* (1480–1950) (Paris: Fayard, 1994), pp. 567–87.

2. A. Jalal, *The Sole Spokesman: Jinnah, the Muslim League and the Demand for Pakistan* (Cambridge: Cambridge University Press, 1985).

3. *See* S. Ansari. 'Partition, Migration and Refugees. Responses to the Arrival of Muhajirs in Sindh during 1947–48', in D.A. Low and H. Brasted (eds), *Freedom, Trauma, Continuities: Northern India and Independence* (New Delhi: Sage, 1998), pp. 91–103.

4. For an analysis of this culture, see D. Chokrabarty, 'Remembered Villages: Representations of Hindu-Bengali Memories in the Aftermath of the Partition', in Low and Brasted, *Freedom, Trauma* ... , op. cit., pp. 133–52.

5. On the literature of Partition, see I. Talbot, 'Literature and the Human Drama of the 1947 Partition', in ibid., pp. 39–55.

6. 'Crosscurrents in the historiography of Partition' (forthcoming).

7. Amongst the abundant literature, let it suffice to mention U. Butalia, 'Community, State and Gender: on women's Agency during Partition', *Economic and Political Weekly*, vol. 18, no. XVII, 24 April 1993; R. Menon and K. Bhasin, 'Recovery, Rupture, Resistance: Indian State and abduction of women during Partition', ibid.; and U. Butalia, *The Other Side of Violence: Voices from the Partition of India* (New Delhi: Viking, 1998).

8. *See* S. Aiyar, '"August Anarchy": The Partition Massacres in Punjab, 1947', in Low and Brasted, *Freedom, Trauma* ... , op. cit., pp. 15–38.

Divorce by Mutual Consent or War of Secession?
(Czechoslovakia–Yugoslavia)*

JACQUES RUPNIK

The simultaneous disappearance, in the aftermath of the collapse of the communist system, of Yugoslavia and Czechoslovakia—two multinational states that were created after the First World War—suggests a number of parallels, but also some questions about their essential difference, namely the fact that in the case of Czechoslovakia the divorce was swift, and took place by mutual consent, whereas in that of Yugoslavia the break-up was violent, and extended over the course of a decade. How is this contrast to be explained if not by vague sweeping statements about differences in political culture between Central Europe and the Balkans, or the evocation of a 'providential figure'—that is, Havel or Milošević who, according to this viewpoint, either warded off or paved the way for a descent into violence.[1]

The destinies of these two multinational states were in many ways parallel: both were offsprings of the Treaty of Versailles, and both made claims to engender a political nation ('Czechoslovakian' and 'Yugoslavian'); but in fact they were dominated, respectively, by Czechs and Serbs. They were both part of the 'little entente', and disappeared in the first instance with the outbreak of the Second World War, whose beneficiaries were, respectively, the Slovaks and the Croats, who created their own states under the patronage of Nazi Germany. At the end of the war, the two states were reconstituted in centralized mode under the aegis of the communist party. They were later

* Translated from the French by John Doherty

federalized: Yugoslavia in two phases, with the Constitutions of 1946 and 1974; Czechoslovakia in 1968, just after the Soviet invasion. The two federations collapsed just after the fall of the communist system at the start of the 1990s, and the word 'federalism' emerged from the communist experience just as discredited as the word 'socialism'. The beginnings of the transition to democracy accelerated the underlying dynamics of centrifugal forces, and founded new legitimacies of power at the level of the republics, to the detriment of the federal power.

The basis of the problem, which was common to both the Czech and Yugoslav failures, was twofold. The first point is that unitary states were built, to begin with, on an ambiguous conception of the 'Czech' and 'Yugoslav' nations, one which did not pre-exist the formation of these states; that is, in neither case did the components belong to the same state before 1918. 'Czechoslovakianism', like 'Yugoslavianism', was less a question of identity than of ideology.[2] The ambiguity of the project lay in the attempt to create political nations on the basis of Czech-Slovak and Serbo-Croat linguistic proximities. This also explains the limits of the project, and its failure. To talk about a 'Czechoslovakian' nation with two branches (Czech and Slovak) made it possible to legitimize the new state in the name of a principle of self-determination, both in the eyes of the outside world and in those of its minorities (German and Hungarian). But the basis of the project turned out to be an illusion: the 'two branches', instead of fusing together, moved apart. Much in the same way, Yugoslavia, in 1918, was 'a Croat idea carried through by Serbian means'; but it came too late to amount to anything other than a juxtaposition of distinct national communities. Centralized conceptions of the state then became a means of making up for these weaknesses, especially in the eyes of the political elites of the dominant nation: the Czechs saw themselves as the torchbearers of a democratic conception of a new state, in which, so to speak, they were giving the Slovaks a share. The Serbs saw themselves as the 'liberators' of the other southern Slavs, and, in this respect, as taking on the mantle of *primus inter pares*. In both cases, this could not but reinforce centrifugal dynamics.

The second reason for the failure had to do with the parallel discrediting of federalism and communism, as well as that of the regime and the state. The federal idea 'seeks to impose the dominance of an association of groups, in a spirit of respect for their specificities, while bringing power closer to the citizen. This type of organization of power is based on the willing cooperation of the authorities, which, vested with primal legitimacy, give up a part of their independence in exchange for liberties that guarantee them a certain legal existence'.[3] The federal system was supposed to represent a permanent quest for consensus and, in this way, to reinforce the legitimacy of the common state, while at the same time recognizing the separate identities of its component parts. It was also supposed to provide a framework for the protection of the rights of national minorities. But a federal state, under communism, obviously could not comply with this democratic dimension of federalism. At most, it could circumscribe conflicts through reinforcing the centralizing, unitary character of the state, if necessary by repressive means, as was the case with the Croat spring of 1971 and the Kosovo crisis of 1981. The fact that the federalization of the Czech state took place in the context of the 'normalization' that followed the crushing of the Prague spring had a decisive influence on its content, and on society's perception of it. Vaclav Havel talked about 'federalized totalitarianism'. In both cases, one could talk about a federation without federalism.

The Absence of a Democratic Alternative

The first consequence of this experiment was that instead of federalism being regarded as a dimension of modern democracy—as in the United States or Western Europe—in Eastern Europe, after 1989, it was perceived as a discredited inheritance of the former communist regime. Instead of trying to reform this institutional structure, or give it a new content, an attempt was made to go beyond it. And this temptation was even stronger in Yugoslavia, given that the decomposition of the communist system in the course of the 1980s went hand in hand with that of the Yugoslavian state. In 1982, Milovan Djilas stated: 'It is not Yugoslavia that is showing signs of falling apart, but the system. There is naturally a danger that the latter may drag the former down with it, if there is no longer the possibility of a democratic alternative.'[4] And this is precisely what happened when the 'democratic alternative' proved impossible to implement across Yugoslavia as a whole, but gained the upper hand, though in no particular pattern, in its constituent republics.

For democracy to have been capable of providing a principle of integration for changeover after the failure of communist integration 'from above', the first democratic elections would have had to take place across the entire Yugoslavian territory. This would have been the only way of legitimizing the territorial framework in which democracy was being introduced. The electoral sequence is of utmost importance for the survival of a multinational state in the process of transition towards democracy.[5] The fact that the first democratic elections were held in the republics as such, and not at the federal level, contributed to the de-legitimizing of the federal state and the transfer of the centre of gravity of political power to the republics. The case of Czechoslovakia shows, however, that the holding of the first free elections on the federal state level was not enough to ensure its survival.[6]

Finally, one of the keys to understanding the failure of the 'federation' concept is the fact that there was an asymmetry of loyalties to the common state. For the Czechs, as for the Serbs, the relationship between national identity and identification with the state was one of symbiosis. This was not the case (or at least not in the same way, or to the same degree) for the Slovaks or the Croats, who were 'junior partners' in the two federations, and had a common history in the Hungarian part of the Hapsburg empire. They had populations of similar size (around five million each), and in both cases Catholicism and national sentiment reinforced each other. Separatism was long discredited by the attempts that had been made to set up separate states during the Second World War. In both cases, the fall of communism was accompanied by an attempt to redefine the constitutional order through a transition from a 'top-down' federal model to a 'bottom-up' confederal model. Instead of asserting an attachment to a common state that would accord a large measure of devolution of power to the constituent republics, it was a question of starting out from the prior recognition of distinct entities which were the depositaries of sovereignty, and which, in a second phase, could agree to delegate a part of this sovereignty (e.g., responsibility for the currency or defence policy) to the common state. In 1990, Croatia and Slovenia held referendums which adumbrated, respectively, the hypotheses of 'dissociation' and 'secession', in case the new confederal arrangement turned out to be impossible. Slovakia did not hold a referendum, but it will be recalled that the parliamentary elections of June 1992 functioned implicitly as such. The winner was Vladimir Meciar's HZDS, which rejected all the constitutional compromises put forward. Its programme was:

1. a declaration of sovereignty by Slovakia (voted in July 1992 by the Slovakian parliament);

2. a Slovakian constitution (adopted in August 1992 by the same people who had rejected all plans for a Czechoslovakian constitution);

3. the election of a Slovakian president (in opposition to the Czechoslovakian president, Vaclav Havel); and

4. the status of Slovakia as a 'subject of international law', with its own diplomatic corps and 'its star on the European flag'.

'Velvet Divorce'/War of Dissolution

The parallels are indeed numerous, but the contrasts are no less so. And these are what make it possible to take account of the essential difference between the Czech-Slovak 'velvet divorce' and the Yugoslavian war of dissolution. If one were to refer only to the constitutional models, the risks of conflict might appear to have been higher in the Czech-Slovak case, given that a bi-polar federation was considered as being non-viable (and in any case a source of conflict). In fact, bi-polar federations tend to become zero-sum games in which any advantage gained by one of the participants is considered as a loss for the other.[7] It is difficult, in such conditions, to formulate a 'common interest' within the political debate; and this, in the end, tends to undermine the legitimacy of the common state.

The case of Yugoslavia was apparently different: as a multinational entity with several actors, and thus multipolar, its modus operandi was comprised of a 'balance of powers' and central arbitrage.[8] 'Cohesion' and control were contributed by the Yugoslavian communist league, and by Tito, who, thanks to his double background in the Hapsburg empire and the communist International, was a past master in the art of creating equilibrium out of repression and concessions, toing and froing between minor and major gestures. After Tito's death, and especially with the accelerating decomposition of the communist system, this equilibrium was torn asunder, firstly, and above all, by the Serbian communist leadership at the end of the 1980s. In fact, it was with the arrival of Slobodan Milošević at the head of the Serbian Communist Party in 1987 that the break with Tito's heritage, and a determination to carry out a 'recentring' in favour of a model that would be more centralized, and more favourable to Serbia, became the motive force in Serbian politics, progressively destabilising relations with the other components of the federation. This is the main explanation for the transition from a model of changing, 'arbitrarily variable' coalitions to an increasing degree of bipolarization, especially between 1989 and 1992. Faced with a pro-Serbian bloc (comprising Serbia and Montenegro, and then also, after Milošević's supporters went into action, Kosovo and Voivodina) which was both in favour of a recentralization of the federation and wary about a 'decommunization' of the regime, there grew up, progressively, a coalition that was favourable to a more confederal, democratic solution. In their opposition to the Serbian hegemony that Milošević represented, Slovenia and Croatia, which went furthest in this direction, were gradually, and hesitantly, joined by Bosnia-Herzegovina and Macedonia, which were accustomed to the idea of an asymmetrical federation, that is, one with differing degrees of integration. It was a common adversary and the escalation of the war that provided the common denominator for this heterogeneous coalition.

Bi-polarity tends to generate disputes, but does not necessarily imply the use of violence. And herein lay the major difference between the two cases: on the one hand, a divorce was worked out in the framework of a transition to democracy which, even if it was sometimes a rocky road, was never called into question by either of the two protagonists, the Czechs and the Slovaks; and on the other hand, in the Serbian case, a contested, distorted transition. It is at this point that the analogy between the Czech Republic and Serbia breaks down. The Czech political entities played a leading role in the democratic transition, whereas Serbia, under Milošević, hindered the dismantling of the communist regime. Where Havel embodied the democratic break with communism, Milošević represented the continuity of a communist apparatus that had converted to nationalism.[9] In the spring of 1991, Havel committed himself to never resorting to force in order to preserve the common state; Milošević, on the other hand, did not hesitate to resort to violence in order to maintain his grasp on power.

While it is true that the Czech Republic did not react to secession in the same way as Serbia, it also has to be admitted that the situation in Slovakia was not the same as in Slovenia or Croatia. In these latter cases, it was possible to talk about small countries that were more prosperous than the rest of the federation, more advanced in the democratic transition, and more firmly attached to Western Europe. But this argument could in no way be applied to Slovakia.

Apart from the relationship to democracy, it was the role of the army that constituted the major explanation for the use of violence, or its absence. Here we had two federal armies fashioned by communist regimes, one of which (i.e., the Czechoslovakian) remained on the sidelines, subordinate to the political process, while the other (i.e., the Yugoslavian) became directly involved in it. In Czechoslovakia, it was hard to see how an army that had not fought to defend the national territory in 1939, after Munich, nor intervened in August 1968 in the face of the Soviet invasion, could take action to defend the common state against an 'internal enemy'. In the

Yugoslavian case, the army had been born out of resistance to an occupant, but also to the nationalist armies. It was thus identified with a Titoesque ethos ('fraternity and unity'). In the Czechoslovakian case, the military were sure of being able to choose the army they wanted for the successor state, whereas in the Yugoslavian case one might, like Ivan Vejvoda, talk about a 'trade dispute', in other words a dispute that was related not only to the defence of a state, but also to threatened status and privileges. In Yugoslavia, the party, like the state, was federalized, and upon the fall of the communist system the army was the only truly supranational institution that could be identified with a federal state in the process of disintegrating. While pro-claiming itself as the ultimate trustee of the heritage of Tito's Yugoslavia, the Yugoslav People's Army definitively betrayed this heritage by making com-mon cause with Milošević's version of it, namely that of bringing all the Serbs together in the same state. 'Between Yugoslavia and communism, it opted for communism. Multi-party politics struck it as suspect, and it rejected the idea. It forgot that it was composed of all the peoples: in the space of a single night, it ceased to be multi-national, and became a pure spark. After that, when the choice was between Yugoslavia and Milošević, it supported Milošević from crime to failure and from failure to crime. It fought against the populations that rejected the power of its favourite son.'[10]

Borders and 'National Minorities'

Finally, and above all: the main difference between Czechoslovakia and Yugoslavia was that of borders and national minorities. In the Yugoslavian case, this was the essential cause of the escalating violence that accompanied the process of secession. The borders of the republics were contested (espe-cially where they had been changed at the time of the liberation), and the non-correspondence of ethnic boundaries with political borders became an argument against their legitimacy. The fact that almost three million Serbs (in other words 40 per cent of the Serbian population of Yugoslavia) lived outside the borders of Serbia seemed acceptable as long as there was the common state of Yugoslavia. If Croatia or Bosnia became independent, the minorities too would proclaim independent 'Serbian republics'. As Vladimir Gligorov said: 'Why should I be a minority in your state when you could be a minority in mine?' The manipulation by Milošević and the Belgrade parties of the 'protection' of Serbian minorities in the republics that opted for independence was one of the main factors that triggered the war in Croatian

Krajina, in 1990–1, and then in Bosnia-Herzegovina—not forgetting Kosovo, where it all began in 1987– 9, and where the war ended ten years later.[11]

The situation was fundamentally different in Czechoslovakia. To begin with, the border between the two republics in question had never been contested. It had existed for a thousand years, between the kingdom of Bohemia and the crown of St Stephen. It is true that there were Czechs living in Slovakia (1 per cent of the population), and Slovaks in Czech territory (around a quarter million), but such people were there for either personal or professional reasons (the federal system had led to many Slovaks working in Prague, either in the army or the state apparatus). These were not 'national minorities' who lived near the border and demanded to be integrated into (or protected by) the mother-nation. In fact the citizens of the 'other' national- ity, in each successor state, were able to live there, and to opt for citizenship.[12] The absence of controversy about either borders or minorities meant that the two main reasons for violence in ex-Yugoslavia were avoided in the case of the Czech-Slovak divorce.

There remains a final reason for the non-violent nature of the Czech- Slovak separation, namely the moderating effect that the war in ex-Yugosla- via exercised over both Prague and Bratislava. During the spring of 1991, the Slovakian press, and the speeches of its politicians, carried references to a process of self-determination, illustrated by the example of the Yugoslav republics ('Slovinsko-Slovenskol?'),[13] but such references disappeared after Vukovar. There had been no serious animosity or history of conflict between Czechs and Slovaks, and there was also the dissuasive effect of the war between the ex-Yugoslavs.

The consequences of a divorce, whether by consent or accompanied by violence, are never without importance. The Czech-Slovak separation weak- ened regional cooperation within the Višegrad group, but did not threaten the stability or security of any neighbouring states, unlike the war in ex- Yugoslavia.[14] And this argument is also relevant to the question of European integration. Slovenia had no Serbian minority, and so it escaped the 'logic of war', which meant that it did not compromise its chances of participating in European integration. In 1997, like the Czech Republic, it was included in the first batch of candidates for the enlargement of the European Union. The transition in Slovakia under Meciar (1992–8) signified a slide towards national-populism (which in many respects was analogous to that of Croatia under Tudjman), and in 1997 Slovakia was excluded from the 'first circle' of potential new members of the EU, though the absence of violence since then, and the existence of a stable, democratic regional environment, have meant that it has once more returned to favour with Europe. After a decade of war, the process will be much slower and more difficult for Yugoslavia's successor states.

Notes

1. V. Havel expressed the contrast in the form of a quip: 'The same thing which in other places—in Russia, or in the Balkans—took the form of an ancient tragedy, in our case was more like the theatre of the absurd, or street theatre, or a farce.' (Le Monde, 3 July 1992).

2. See S. Pavlowitch. 'Yougoslavie: de l'idéal de l'Etat-nation à la barbarie des pouvoirs ethniques', in J. Rupnik (ed.), Le déchirement des nations (Seuil: Paris, 1995), p. 80.

3. M. Gjidara, 'La solution fédérale: bilan critique', in Pouvoirs, no. 57, spring 1991, p. 93.

4. Interview with J. Rupnik in L'Alternotive, September–October 1982, p. 55.

5. Cf. J.-J. Linz and A. Stepan, 'Political identities and electoral sequences: Spain, the Soviet Union, and Yugoslavia', in Daedalus, spring 1992, pp. 123–40.

6. For an analysis of the reasons behind the Czech-Slovak breakup, see J. Rupnik, 'Le divorce tchécoslovaque', in Critique Internationale, no. 3, 1999.

7. See F. Delpérée's argument, 'Le fédéralisme sauvera-t-il la nation belge?' in J. Rupnik (ed.), Le déchirement des nations (Seuil: Paris, 1995), pp. 123–38. The case of Czechoslovakia is similar to that of Belgium and Canada.

8. See S. P. Ramet, Nationalism and federalism in Yugoslavia, 1962–1991 (Bloomington: Indiana University Press, 1992).

9. Regarding Milošević's takeover of Serbian nationalism, see V. Stevanović, Milošević une épitaphe (Paris: Fayard, 2000). This book, which is the most important by a leading Serbian intellectual, was published in September 2000. It received no reviews in Belgrade after the fall of Milošević.

10. V. Stevanović, ibid., p. 327.

11. See Independent International Commission on Kosovo, Kosovo, Report, Conflict, International Response, Lessons Learned (Oxford: Oxford University Press, 2000).

12. The problem was, nonetheless, a real one for the Roms of Slovakia who arrived in the Czech Republic at the time of the break-up, fearing the nationalists excesses of the Meciar regime, or those who did not choose Czech nationality during the year that followed the separation.

13. This is what M. Kraus and A. Stanger call the 'demonstration effect', that is, the impact of international processes on internal Czech dynamics; in M. Kraus and A. Stanger (eds), *Irreconcilable Differences? Explaining Czechoslovakia's Dissolution* (Lanham: Rowman & Littlefield Publishers, 2000), p. 17.

14. See 'Le dialogue des sept Presidents', *in Transeuropéennes*, no. 3; also Anne Nivat, 'Le quatuor de Višegrad', *in Transeuropéennes*, no. 1.

On the Hague Conference, 1991*

GORAN FEJIĆ

Ten years have elapsed since the conclusion of the Conference on Yugoslavia in The Hague, a well-intentioned but ill-fated initiative of emerging European foreign policy. With the help of Sonja Biserko, my friend and colleague at the former Federal Secretariat of Foreign Affairs, I was once again able to get my hands on the proceedings from the Conference held from 7 September to 18 October 1991. The Conference was the European Community's final attempt to counter the logic of war and ethno-territorial divisions in the Balkans, with the idea of preserving the Yugoslav space and opening the perspective of its integration into the Community. ('We are gathered here to give reason a chance', said the Chairman of the European Community Council, Dutch Minister of Foreign Affairs Van den Broek, at the opening). On the Yugoslav side, such assistance was called for and expected by the Federal Government of Ante Marković, hoping that it might help curb rising nationalism and stop the destruction of war. For integration into Europe was, at the time, the declared goal of all the Yugoslav republics, whether the integration was conceived as individual as in Slovenia or within the frame-work of the broader Yugoslav community. The European Community's standpoint shifted during The Hague Conference, moving from resolute support for the preservation of Yugoslavia's integrity[1] to the final proposal, which called for the 'recognition of the independence of those seeking independence and the free association of those who want it'. As can easily be concluded from the reports and numerous statements made by European diplomats/statesmen at that time, this shift in position was primarily the

* Translated from the Serb-Croatian by Teodora Tabački

outcome of 'developments on the ground'—that is, in the war that was spreading inexorably ...

As the head of the Department for European Integration at the Federal Secretariat for Foreign Affairs, I participated in the sessions of The Hague Conference as a member of the Federal Government's delegation. Amongst other things, my duty was to write up short reports immediately after the sessions. Much to my surprise, the contents of those reports never led to any comment or sign of discontent from the belligerent participants. As I later understood, that did not mean they agreed with the content of those reports, but simply that they never read them, that they were utterly indifferent— another sign that for them the conference was in no way a place for seeking compromise, but a forum for confronting immutable convictions. By defini- tion, taking notes is not an especially creative job. I tried to do it properly, however, neither changing nor valorising the meaning of what was said. I believed that I was taking part in an event crucial for the future of my country—and thus for my own future. At the same time, I felt utterly helpless. My United Nations experience offered me some hope: the meeting's co-ordinator had the opportunity to clearly state the issues, and being in a position of power could help bring about mutual concessions and a sort of— albeit imposed—compromise.

We travelled to The Hague in a small Federal Government aircraft. Only the delegations from Croatia and Slovenia flew separately in their own planes from Zagreb and Ljubljana. The members of Presidency travelled with their bodyguards. The conversation on the small plane was minimal and the atmosphere dreadful. During the first half hour, we looked at villages burning in Slavonia. One of those flights, particularly the landing in The Hague, has remained deeply engraved in my memory. Night was falling. The picture through the window was extremely beautiful: far away, the sea was still shimmering silver. Closer, beneath the plane, on the already dark surface of the earth, we could see the contours of the glass roofs of greenhouses, glowing like luminous cubes. The surface of the Netherlands offered visual harmony of nature and the work of human hands. When it was explained to him what the big shining squares were, one of the bodyguards commented: 'God damn, those would make bloody good targets for our artillery!'

The Hague milieu was surrealist—particularly given the tragic back- ground of the war. Somewhere between an Enki Bilal cartoon and an Almodovar film. In the hypermodern building of the Dutch Foreign Ministry— architecturally closer to a hotel at Miami Beach than state-administration headquarters—the delegation of each republic had its own separate office. The hosts' exaggerated kindness was visible at every turn: in the huge lobby, just by the conference hall, gigantic flower decorations and a plentiful buffet at lunch time. To and fro on that hospitable stage walked the sullen-faced heads of the emerging Balkans ethnocracies.

At no point did the Hague Conference succeed in 'controlling' the situation on the ground, but remained on the contrary hostage of that situation right to the end. The European Community first tried to get consent on the basic principles of negotiation (which were at the same time to be the principles for any future arrangement of the Yugoslav space): i) there were to be no unilateral border changes, especially not through the use of force; ii) the rights of all[2] in Yugoslavia were to be protected; iii) all[2] legitimate interests and aspirations were to be taken into consideration. However, with the escalation of war in Croatia, the debate on essential issues concerning the future was endlessly delayed. The participants gave their own, contradictory versions of what was happening on the ground. For the Community, the cease-fire became the top priority. The conference bogged down and the Chairman, Lord Carrington, tried to break the deadlock with a trilateral meeting between the war's leading protagonists—Tudjman, Milošević and General Kadijević. At the meeting in Igalo, all three solemnly accepted the committment 'that all forces under their command, or under their political and military influence, would immediately cease fire and undertake other measures against the recurrence of armed conflicts'. In order to intensify the Conference's work on crucial issues, expert groups were set up on economic issues, future institutions and their structure, and human and minority rights. In early October, just prior to the Conference's fourth session, fighting in Croatia escalated again. On 4 October, having totally usurped the Yugoslav National Army, turning it into an instrument of bloodshed, the Milošević regime and the so-called 'Serb block', took control of the Presidency of the SFRY, an act interpreted by the European Community as an infringement of the Constitution, while the Federal Government of Ante Marković called it an inacceptable act. Finally, on 18 October, given the utter deadlock of negotiations and further escalation of war, the Community called for a second meeting at the highest level, where Carrington gave his final proposal of an 'arrangement for a general solution' along the following lines:

• all those republics who so desired could become sovereign and independent states, recognized by the international community;

- those who desired to join together were free to do so;
- arrangements and mechanisms for monitoring human rights were to be set up;
- certain groups and regions were to enjoy special status;
- Europe asserted its commitment to reaching these agreements and to recognizing the independence of the states desiring it within the framework of existing frontiers, except in the case of different agreements between republics.

The proposal further elaborated dispositions for the protection of human rights and the rights of national minorities and ethnic groups. In other words, the proposal said: 'If you are not capable of living together, separate peacefully, maintain a minimum level of communication between yourselves, as well as a common economic space, with mutual guarantees of basic human rights for national minorities.'

Today, I am able to judge those times from a different perspective. Responsibilities for the crimes committed are clearer, but so are the meanderings of the international community, which lacked both the wisdom and the resolve to stop the criminals in time. In successive phases of the Balkan wars, it became evident that European foreign policy was still in its swaddling clothes and that humanitarian action often masks a lack of political strategy (the clearest examples being the three years of atrocious shelling of besieged Sarajevo, the systematic destruction of Mostar, and the UN's incapacity to defend the civilians in the so-called safe areas). Now that we know the mechanisms for inciting ethnic hatred, and now that the plans for ethnic cleansing and the secret Milošević–Tudjman deals for the partition of Bosnia have come to light, Van den Broek's appeals to the Yugoslav participants for reason at the opening of the Conference seem naive and useless. As does his quote from Jean Monnet, one of the spiritual fathers of the European Community: 'We should not fight for national frontiers, but rather make them unimportant through intensified economic and political cooperation, in order to finally remove them'. Alas! The very day after the Conference opened, the shelling of towns in Croatia continued, along with conquering territories, slaughter, and ethnic cleansing. Shooting and negotiating cannot go together, pleaded Van den Broek, if you want the Conference to be fruitful, the fighting has to stop immediately! The fighting did not cease. On the contrary, with every new session, peace became an ever more distant goal, as did the preservation of any common economic, cultural, or political

space for the Yugoslav nations. It grew harder for the European Community to advocate the idea that aggressor and victim should continue to live together. Croatia was at the time obviously in the position of a victim and it is only with the war in Bosnia that it became clear how the victim itself can become an aggressor in the partition of a new prey.

One part of my country was at war against the other. Day after day, I felt more and more a stranger there.

Today, we can contemplate the Hague Conference from several different perspectives. That of the citizens of the successor states of the former Yugoslavia, for instance. What would have happened if the European Community's proposals had been accepted—the proposals aiming at a free association or peaceful separation of those states, yet with the maintenance of normal human, cultural, and economic relations within the common Yugoslav space?

Let us leave aside for a moment the most important thing, which understandably first comes to mind: the fact that war would have been avoided along with its most tragic consequences: hundreds of thousands of victims, millions of displaced people, psychological trauma and wounds that will take generations to heal. Following upon years of killing and destruction comes the misery, material poverty and cultural impoverishment, isolation, xenophobia, and collective paranoia. How would it be were it not for all of that? Let us try to imagine. What would we have instead of the present Balkans, crumbled into tiny, economically dysfunctional and culturally crippled pseudo-states in constant conflict, condemned to remain the patients of the international community (some of the patients are already undergoing treatment, receiving transfusions, others are only now leaving the quarantine, waking from their drunken ten-year coma, denouncing their adulated war-criminal leader, whom they democratically elected several times in a row. Ten years after the 'emergence of the people' we are witnessing the emergence of citizens. The latter process, however, is slower than the former. One's dignity as a citizen has to be re-established before others as well as before oneself. The Tudjman era in Croatia is more and more often put into question. In Serbia, Milošević has fallen, the first steps have finally been taken, there is hope. But the hardest part is still to come: the sobering up of all those who blindly followed the chieftain for thirteen years running. Facing themselves, recognizing their hung-over faces, covered with blood, addressing their own children, explaining what happened, exposing themselves to their judgement, letting them turn and choose something different. Questions have to

be answered: what were you doing while Vukovar, Sarajevo, and Mostar were being demolished? Or during the massacre in Srebrenica? All of that is possible, but it takes time and courage. Other European peoples walked that road half a century ago, and new generations have recovered their dignity. And they did so not by forgetting the past, but by looking it straight in the eye, acknowledging it as their own in its superlatively detestable form, condemning it before the world and thereby accomplishing redemption. That is why the Hague Tribunal has an immense symbolic value. It was a mistake not to indict Tudjman as well, but that does not diminish the importance of the indictments against Milošević and his crew. The Hague convictions are not only important as a response to the widows and mothers of all those killed in Srebrenica. They could primarily help the citizens of Serbia, even Croatia, in the painful sobering that is ahead. That sobering is not only a precondition for European integration, but for all that is presently meant by the term 'transition': building a credible state, based on the rule of law, an independent legal system and other democratic institutions, an economic system based on the pursuit of welfare for oneself and family, along with the complex interaction of rights and obligations, a culture of negotiating and reaching agreements, respect for the Other and seeking the minimal common denominator of social interests. All of which is very far from the rule of smugglers and the financial Mafia currently plaguing the Balkans and the greater part of Eastern Europe, where the powerful impose their will through blackmail and threat, while the silent majority suffers and merely survives.

And if the last round of Balkan wars had been avoided (as it could have been), the hardest part of the 'transition' (i.e., adapting to the new democratic game rules), would most likely have been overcome. Ten years have passed—a long period indeed. With no exaggeration, it is safe to presume that the Yugoslav space would by now already be a part of the European Community, which would of course have made it irrelevant whether that space was federal, confederal, or made up of an association of states. Having recovered their capacity to think rationally, people would have realized that nationalism was a lure and that the notion of sovereignty is becoming increasingly relative, particularly in the field of the economy. In economic terms, the sovereignty of France or Italy is seriously limited by the rules applying to the Fifteen. Although those rules raise questions (above all with regard to their discriminatory effects on third countries), there can be no doubt that they open space for development and cultural interaction and

enrichment for citizens of the Community, which would be inconceivable within the frontiers of their nation states. At the time of its suicide, Yugoslavia was at the very doorstep of the European Community. Already in the early eighties, the former SFRY had an economy almost entirely based on Western technology, liberal international trade, and legislation regarding intellectual property compatible with European norms. It was already a country with a significant middle class, a solid system of public education, culturally open to the rest of the world. In a word, it was the country with the best chances for a relatively painless and easy 'transition'. Ante Marković's government was about to close an agreement with the European Community far more ambitious than the deals recently made by some of the eastern European states. Yugoslavia (that is, the real Yugoslavia, stretching from Triglav to Gjevgjelia—the only one which is not usurping the name), could by now have reached a good medium-level of development—be it as a confederation or as an association of states—better integrated into Europe than Portugal or Greece, with extraordinary potential in terms of transport, tourism, and new technologies, as well as every right to use all available European funds for regional development. Initially, the European Community insisted upon only two conditions, neither of which was insurmountable, given Yugoslavia's level of political and social development: free, multi-party elections at the Federal level and adequate guarantees regarding the respect of human rights (including, of course, the rights of all minorities). As is well known, no federal election has ever taken place. Marković's attempt to stop the nationalist madness, by creating his own reformist party, came too late. Milošević had already devised his war scenario, while Tudjman had successfully capitalized on Serbian threats and the exacerbated nationalism in Krajina, Slavonia, and Bosnia. Croatian nationalism could have found no better fuel for its own outburst. The fact that it caught on in a country that was at the same time the victim of aggression, made it no less exclusive, virulent, and warmongering. By the autumn of 1991, identity resentments had reached the point where no rational argument could work any longer. The Hague Conference was a last-ditch effort. Its failure is just another example of the helplessness of reason in the face of bewildering fury.

From the perspective of the European (and more broadly international) community, the most interesting question is: had we known then whom we were dealing with, which strategy would we have used?

As already mentioned, at no point during the course of the Hague Conference did combat in the country ever stop. The concomitance of warfare and negotiation had two consequences:

- the first had to do with the roles of negotiators: the Community focused attention on the warmongers instead of the members of those delegations (Federal Government, Bosnia and Herzegovina, Macedonia) willing to help seek consensus. Thus, Milošević: and Tudjman took on greater importance, pushing the other negotiators, above all the Federal Government, into the background;

- the second has to do with the very content and course of negotiations: against the background of intensifying war and destruction, peace, in its most elementary sense as cease-fire, becomes the most urgent objective. All considerations about the coherent and rational framework for the development of the Yugoslav space and long-term European integration are set aside. As the shelling of Dubrovnik, Osijek, and Vukovar reached it height, the European public quickly began to choose to support the victim. More and more voices demanded recognition for the independence of Croatia, Slovenia and the other republics 'who so desired it'. That was the essence of Carrington's proposal, with insistence on respective obligations of all republics regarding the upholding of human and minority rights.

At first glance, the proposal is compatible with the basic criteria of common sense. Unfortunately, the recognition of the new states failed to stop the aggression led by the Serbian and Yugoslav Army, nor did Europe understand that multiethnic Bosnia and Herzegovina could not be divided along ethnic lines. Europe was in a schizophrenic position: on the one hand, it was trying to assert its role in its own backyard, proving itself to be a new player on the post-Cold War global scene; and on the other, it had neither the firepower nor the political will (nor probably the support of its own public opinion) to consistently back the principles that are allegedly at its foundation. In the thick fog of diplomatic improvisation, the notion of an ethnic war was invoked, as an allegedly new phenomenon,[3] drawing its force from irreducible ethnic, religious, and cultural differences. Images were served to public opinion carrying an implicit message: no one can be blamed for failure when ancestral hatreds, the forces of nature itself are confronted. The public, however, still demanded that something be done, as pictures of slaughter and destruction became unbearable: 'For Christ's sake, we are not talking about Africa here, but a country where we go on holiday, only an hour or two away from the European capitals.' Skilled analysts were called upon to explain that

those Balkan nations are in fact in constant conflict, that clashes of civilizations always take place in that territory (Eastern and Western Roman
Empire, Austro-Hungarian and Ottoman Empires, etc.) and that the conflicts were only ever suppressed by the iron fist of Tito. In a single gesture, the
Yugoslav people's seventy years of common history was erased, the circumstances and ideas from which the Yugoslav movement emerged more than a
century ago were forgotten, and Yugoslavia was declared an artificial creation of Versailles. And so on. But, the greatest gain of declaring an 'ethnic'
war was the abdication of responsibility: as 'ethnic war' was waged not on
principles, but in the name of God-given opposition between nations, any
outside intervention misses the point. Politics yields to genetics. There is,
therefore, neither justice nor blame, and war for the contested area becomes
somehow 'natural', the major question becoming how to protect oneself from
the contagious disease; how to make sure that those 'ethno-states' stay
outside, away from the European realm, where crime has to be stopped and
victims protected, the realm in which public authorities have to uphold the
law and its credibility; how to efficiently protect Europe from barbarism,
rejecting all that could remind it of what it once was and is today ashamed of
and disgusted with. However, the European voters were upset with the
virtual war in their homes, European governments felt public pressure that
something be done; European humanism, it was felt, ought to be demonstrated. Humanitarian action came to the fore. Humanitarian organizations
brought food and medicine to civilians who were already—or soon would
be—expelled, raped, and robbed. At the same time, the divorce of the
'ethnic groups' continued unabated, driven by the principle that might
makes right. Warmongers were very well aware of that and continued to lie
and sign cease-fires while at the same time plotting new war plans. First they
shaped Great Serbia, then Greater Croatia. Thus, step by step, their international profiles evolved. At the beginning, they were negociators on the
urgent cease-fire issue. Gradually, they became accepted as negotiators on
the future organization of the Yugoslav space.

It took ten years for the world to grasp that the nature of evil was political,
not ethnic. Aggressive nationalism was finally wearing itself out, after it had
worn out all the myths and shown that it couldn't produce anything but vain
hatred and misery. Europe is paying a steep price for its short-sightedness.
Instead of a strong and reliable partner, it has an unstable and inflammable
area for a neighbour, in need of constant surveillance. Both the peacekeeping

forces and aid programmes devour millions of dollars. The establishment of a cordon sanitaire, aimed at stopping the uncontrolled influx of refugees has fared no better. Thousands of refugees from the Balkans—displaced people searching for safer homes—were not to be discouraged by any Schengen treaty. Of course, neither Europe nor the world are to blame for what happened to us. But they are responsible for not doing all they could to oppose the evil by all means, while it was still possible to do so. Perhaps the fate of the Balkans would have been different if the aggressive nationalism had been deprived of all legitimacy ten years ago; if it had been named for what it really was—racism and fascism; if all contacts with its agents had been cut off; if the non-nationalist reformers had been backed politically and economically. It is hard to speculate about that today. One thing, though, is sure: fifty years after the Second World War, preoccupied with its own prosperity and inner disputes (common agricultural policy, trade and monetary policy, the Schengen treaty, and so on) Europe has begun to forget—to downgrade the anti-fascist values that were at its root. Generation gaps have ruptured historical memory, and even the final consequences of segregation—be it national, ethnic, religious, racial, gender-based or other—have been forgotten.

In the minds of a large number of benevolent European citizens, democracy has progressively been reduced to electoral procedure.[4] The latter, of course, is necessary and there is no democracy without it; but it is also insufficient. It should not be forgotten that both Milošević and Tudjman were elected in multi-party democratic elections, and that no one—either locally or internationally—contested their legitimacy when they thus came to power. In fact, it is partly due to their electoral legitimacy that both Europe and the international community at large accepted them as interlocutors, giving them preference over Ante Marković, who was formally a member of the old socialist nomenclature, though essentially a far more authentic democrat and reformer. I believe that learning from such experiences, the European Union imposed last year's sanctions on Austria, establishing a threshold that must not be crossed if one wants to be a member of the democratic community. I also believe that the recent abolishment of those sanctions was an error, trivializing racist discourse as if it were an attitude just like any other, undesirable for the majority, but still not nasty enough to warrant excommunication. If the Balkan war chieftains had been excommunicated in time, the Balkans might have looked different today. It is hard to say whether Europe drew any moral consequences from it all. Based on the positions it advocates today in support of interculturalism in Bosnia, the preservation of Bosnia and Herzegovina's integrity and in opposition to the ethnic partition of Kosovo, it seems that it did. But its lack of resolve in imposing those positions and its hasty renouncement of the demand for Milošević's extradition to the ICTY would testify to the contrary.

Lastly, for many citizens of the former Yugoslavia, the Hague Conference marked the beginning of the bloody end of the only country they felt to be their own, be it because they were children from mixed marriages and raised in several cultures, be it because by living in various towns and republics, they came to feel equally at home in Belgrade, Zagreb, or Sarajevo, or simply they never felt one piece of their former homeland as more of their own than the others. Some went abroad, starting new lives as stateless people; others stayed in Belgrade, Zagreb, Ljubljana, as strangers in their new, closed-in and claustrophobic, ethnically homogenous surroundings. They continue to cultivate their cross-border friendships, read books published in what are now neighbouring states. In Zagreb, they are contemptuously referred to as 'Yugo-nostalgics'. In Belgrade, the insult they have to suffer is worse still (even on the tongues of benevolent, non-nationalist people), for today's Serbia and Montenegro are persistently referred to by the name of that late, slaughtered country: Yugoslavia. No geographical or historical reason can justify the maintenance of that name. We are dealing here both with a logical absurdity and an usurpation, by means of which the Milošević regime sought to impose the idea that Serbia and Montenegro were Yugoslavia's only successors. This has double implications: on the one hand, the issue is one of legacy over the possessions of the former Yugoslavia; on the other hand, a dangerous confusion is created between nations (Serbs and Montenegrins in this case) and the territory claimed. Those citizens of former Yugoslavia who refused to define themselves ethnically were stripped not only of their country but, worse still, of the name of their country. Other former Yugoslav republics did nothing to oppose that, either through ignorance or in their own nationalist blindness and desire to symbolically 'split from Yugoslavia'. The international community remained indifferent. We wish we could hope that the new democratic regime in Serbia will adopt a more honest approach to the issue and cease to usurp the name of Yugoslavia.

Notes

1. During the summer of 1991, the European Community adopted several

resolutions stating that 'a united and democratic Yugoslavia' had the best chances to integrate itself within the European Community.

2. The term 'all' was intended to refer to citizens, nations, ethnic groups, and minorities and, especially, to avoid Byzantine discussions among Yugoslav negotiators as to who was a minority and who was not.

3. As if ethnic intolerance and racism had not been important features in previous wars.

4. See *Transeuropéennes* no. 17, 'La Fragilité démocratique'. (editors' note)

Refugee Memory in India and Pakistan

SYED SIKANDER MEHDI

'Only through remembrance can painful memories be forgotten.'

Edward Said

Once a refugee, always a refugee. Like death, memory of uprooting, flight, refuge, return or settlement abroad cannot be wished away. Further, irrespective of the legal status acquired—refugee, state less, returnee, asylee, exilee, new settler, citizen of a new country—one continues to frequent the hall of horrors which is very often what the refugee's past amounts to. There is no escape from this past, it has to be lived and relived and that is all there is to it.

Post-Partition refugee life for the millions of Hindus, Sikhs, and Muslims living in India and Pakistan is no different. They live in memory and memory lives in them. The bitter past is always there with them. In the process, the memory of refugeehood has become concretized, structured, and rooted—making healing very difficult. It is, after all, not easy for the victims to forget the bleeding past and forgive those who looted and plundered, committed rape and murder of near and dear ones, and inflicted forced migration.

Healing becomes all the more difficult in India and Pakistan where diverse and powerful interest groups have benefited from the business of conflict between the two post-colonial South-Asian states and where a culture of hate has been deliberately promoted on both sides of the borders—

* An earlier draft of this paper was submitted at the International Summer School on Forced Migration, organized at Oxford, UK, by the Refugee Studies Centre, Oxford University, 17 July–04 August 2000.

borders drawn, moreover, in blood. As such, it is in the interest of these groups that conflicts remain and spread, that hate and fear proliferate, that Partition wounds fester, and that refugee memory continue to inflame passion, hatred, and intolerance. Therefore, the power elites in both countries dedicatedly, carefully, and systematically craft refugee memory, fitting it into the wider scheme of things in order to rationalize hatred, warriorism, militarism, nuclearism, and religious intolerance in the post-Partition subcontinent.

Viewed from a humanitarian perspective, the use of refugee memory for hate-sustenance, mistrust-building, and conflict-perpetuation is highly unethical, to say the least. It is also unacceptable to humanitarian and refugee law and to the international human rights regime. Finally, more than fifty years after Partition, the victim generation is fast disappearing in both the countries, whereas the post-Partition generations—growing up in the post-Cold War era and in an age of disappearing borders within the European Union—have a rather detached view of things which happened long ago. They are reluctant to subscribe to the official viewpoint on conflicts and carnage and tend to romanticize peace not war, harmony not disharmony, co-operation not confrontation, and forgiveness not revenge.

Hence, even if the dominant view in both India and Pakistan continues to be communal and rooted in the politics of blaming and blackening the other, a humanitarian perspective—a holistic people's perspective—is clearly emerging. There is growing interest in Partition today—not so much in the history of Partition, but in what Ranabir Samaddar calls 'the history that Partition creates'[1] or what Ian Talbot describes as the human dimension of the Partition.[2] Also noticeable is the fresh quest for a past—not a rogue past, but a more holistic, more non-communal past.

Memory and Reconciliation

What role can refugee memory play in this quest? Can refugee memory play a positive role, a trust-building role, a reconciliation-promoting role, in short, a healing role in a subcontinent which has suffered from the wounds of Partition for over fifty years?

Here at the very outset, one may point out that among the four famous twentieth-century partitions—Ireland, India, Palestine, and Cyprus, all of which were accompanied by wholesale violence and large-scale population displacements—the Partition of India caused the greatest migration in human history. Never before or since have so many people exchanged their homes and countries so fast. In the span of just a few months in 1947, as many as twelve million people moved between new India and newly created Pakistan.

By far the largest proportion of these refugees—more than ten million—crossed the Western border that divided the province of Punjab. Here, Muslims travelled west to Pakistan and Hindus and Sikhs east to India. In between, on the roads, in the paddy fields, and on the railway tracks awaited violence, rape, and death for Hindus, Muslims, and Sikhs. In only three months, between August and October 1947, the entire Punjab was seized by a communal civil war involving some of the largest ethnic-cleansing campaigns in history. Estimates of death caused by slaughter, malnutrition, and contagious diseases vary between 200,000 (the British estimate at the time) and two million (a later Indian speculation). The generally accepted figure is somewhere around one million.

The Partition carnage was a free-for-all. Members of all three dominant religious communities—Hindus, Muslims, and Sikhs—participated in both pre- and post-Partition orgies of violence. In March 1947, for instance, some 40,000 Sikhs were affected because of disturbances in the Multan, Mianwali, Jhelum, Attock, and Rawalpindi districts of West Punjab. They had to take refuge in the hurriedly established camps and were later sent to safety in Amritsar. Similarly, on 26 October 1946—several months before Partition—the Hindus began attacks on the Muslims in Bihar. The riots then spread to the entire Monghyr district, and within one month, over 100,000 people suffered displacement. By the end of November, more than 400 Muslims had crossed the provincial boundary and taken shelter in Bengal.[3] After Partition, in particular, the well-armed and organized Shahidi Jathas[4] attacked not only Muslim villages, but also trains packed with refugees heading toward Pakistan. In one incident alone, an attack on a train just outside Khalsa College, Amritsar, resulted in the massacre of one thousand Muslims.

The Muslims, likewise, attacked Hindus and Sikhs living in West Punjab, as well as those travelling to India. On 25–6 August, for example, in Sheikhupura—where there was a Muslim majority—looting, killing, and burning continued for twenty-four hours, and two wells in the Namdhari Gurdwara (Sikhs' worship house) were filled with the bodies of Hindu and Sikh women who, to avoid assault, had committed suicide. Refugee trains carrying Hindus and Sikhs were frequently and brutally attacked by the Muslims especially from Raiwind, Wazirabad, and Narowal; the railway tracks between Sialkot and Amritsar were often strewn with the dead bodies of Sikhs.

Government functionaries dealing with law-and-order situations were frequently rendered dysfunctional and powerless. The local warlords were supreme, and before the British had even left, the Indian police was communalized, its intelligence forces broken down, and morale and discipline amongst officials was in sharp decline. Ian Talbot points out that in districts like 'Jallundhar, power consequently lay not with the deputy commissioner, but with Sikh committees of action', forcing Muslims to fall 'prey to the wiles of such Sikh landlords as Raja Bachan Singh'. The Sikh landlord, he adds, had initially promised protection for the 1200 Muslims in the village of Rorka Kalan, but later ordered them to demolish their mosques and convert to Sikhism. Again, according to eye-witness accounts, the police had lost all discipline in the East Punjab and on numerous occasions engaged in rape, looting, and killing. One report says that police Sub-Inspector Sampuran Singh led an attack on 3 September 1947, massacring three hundred Muslims from Hansi in the Hissar District; Sita Ram, the Deputy Superintendent of police in Ambala, supervised attacks on Muslims, including a brutal raid on a refugee train on 15 September claiming a thousand lives.[5]

Women's Memory

Women, on both sides of the borders suffered enormously both during and after the Partition carnage. Some 100,000 women were abducted, mainly in the Punjab. These were Hindu, Muslim, and Sikh women who were raped by men of religions different from their own. Many were killed. Many were sold into prostitution. Others were sold from hand to hand. A number of abducted women were taken as wives and married by conversion; still others just went missing. Many among them witnessed the killing of their near and dear ones before or after suffering sexual assault.

According to Khurshed Mehta, who served as a medical welfare worker in 1947—meeting the refugee trains as they arrived from Punjab at Old Delhi Station—almost half the women she helped were virtually destitute, and had been assaulted. 'The main aim', Khurshed says, 'was to rescue the women and see that they didn't go astray. All these brothel people would wait at the platform trying to grab them. We had to make sure they were not taken away'. Women, as Urvashi Butalia points out, were most at risk while on the move:

When people started to move, either on foot or by train or in buses, that's when women were abducted. In the big caravans, they would get left behind. They couldn't keep up. They had children to look after. Even to use the toilet, women had to go off on their own. They would be abducted from the edges of these big columns. They would be pulled off trains.[6]

Indeed, the foot columns presented the most pathetic aspects of sub-continental refugeehood. Comprising men, women, and children, these terror-stricken, sometimes malnourished, exhausted, refugees moved by the thousands and were exposed to multiple vulnerabilities on their way to their new homeland. Between 18 September and 29 October 1947, observes Randhawa, over 800,000 people, with hundreds of bullock carts and cattle, crossed over to India from the Lyallpur, Montgomery, and Sheikhupura districts. Likewise, on the day of 5 September alone, 50,000 Muslim refugees arrived in Kasur on foot from Ferozepure district. The plight of such people on the move has been well depicted by Kartar Singh Duggal, a prominent Sikh fiction writer of India. Towards the close of his famous novel on Partition and migration entitled *Twice-Born, Twice-Dead*, he presents a poignant picture of a Muslim refugee column passing through Amritsar. Described by Ian Talbot as a piece of 'inestimable value to the historian concerned with understanding the Partition experience "from beneath"', one passage reads:

A caravan of Muslim evacuees was on the move. Whenever such a caravan was to pass, the police usually clamped down a curfew ... Policemen lined both sides of the road to prevent incidents. Still the Hindu shopkeepers and their children poked fun at the cowed, miserable, hungry and emaciated evacuees. The caravan was moving. Bullock carts were loaded with boxes, trunks and spinning wheels. On the top were charpoys, bedding and sacks. On the sacks were old men and women carrying fowls, cats and lambs. From the bullock carts hung hubble-bubbles, baskets, prayer mats, odds and ends. Holding on to the bullock carts for imaginary support walked women with babies at their breasts. Muslim women nurtured behind seven veils ran the gauntlet of hostile glances. The men were wounded, they had seen their relatives hacked to pieces with kirpans. There was not a single young man in the column ... There were small boys, bare-footed, bare-headed, walking fast or slowing down to cast a longing glance at the hot jalebies in the sweet shops. The most yearning look however was cast at the running tap ... No Muslim dared to take a drop of water from the Hindu tap. Men, women and children looked beseechingly at the water flowing from the tap and moved on.[7]

Past Plural

Such was the horrendous past reality of refugeehood on both sides of the borders. This past has lingered on for a long time. But was it the only past there was? Or was there another past as well?

'The image of the past', observes distinguished Indian historian Romila Thapar, 'is the historian's contribution to the future.'[8] But, by and large, both Indian and Pakistani historians have simply ignored the Partition holocaust or have made mere passing references to the wounds of Partition. They focused on the power game played by the British, the Congress, and the Muslim League. Those who focused on the human dimensions of the Partition were often swayed away by communal passion and deep-rooted resentment; in their religious zeal, history was reduced to vendettas. Many in Pakistan and India presented particularizing, communalizing, and dehumanizing perspectives of Partition. They projected the image of a past which was worse than the past itself and made the future no less dehumanizing. They identified victims as well as perpetrators of violence on purely communal lines. For a Hindu or Sikh historian, the Muslims were the perpetrators of violence, and Partition carnage meant the murder and rape of the Hindus and Sikhs by the Muslims—and that was all. Likewise, for a Muslim historian, all Muslims were good, whereas all Hindus and Sikhs were devils, and Partition carnage meant the murder and rape of Muslims by Hindus and Sikhs. Hence, the past was brutalized and divided along communal lines by the post-Partition historians, politicians, government functionaries, media people, and other public-opinion leaders. Subsequently, the future was similarly divided and brutalized along the same lines.

But clearly there was another past—a past which was humane and harmonizing, even during the worst moments of communal frenzy—both before and after Partition. Though neither properly documented nor projected, the fact of the matter is that Hindus and Muslims lived in harmony in many areas of many villages and towns in India and Pakistan, both immediately before and immediately after 1947. There were places where Indian and Pakistani flags were hoisted in the houses of the Hindus and Muslims in close proximity and no violence ensued. Again, while many Hindu, Sikh, and Muslim families panicked and took flight in haste—having no time to properly organize their departure—there were many of those who consulted their friends belonging to the other religious community and often left their homes and hearth for the new homeland with the assistance—and under the protection—of the people belonging to the other community. For many, the migration was a sort of tearing of the people from their lands and roots; the longing for the lost home is present among many surviving refugees—and even among the next generation of refugees.

Another aspect begging for special mention is the fact that both the governments of India and Pakistan, headed respectively by Jawahar Lal Nehru and Liaquat Ali Khan, did work very hard to control post-Partition communal violence, and extensively co-operated with each other to protect human lives, provide shelter to the threatened, arrange rail and road transports with escorts to hundreds of thousands of Muslims, Sikhs, and Hindus migrating from India to Pakistan and from Pakistan to India. The officials often organized joint patrolling in the most sensitive areas. Nehru and Liaquat, for instance, visited Amritsar in Indian Punjab and issued a joint statement on 18 August 1947, expressing their determination to suppress disorder and restore peace and security. On 29 August, the Joint Defence Council for India and Pakistan decided to abolish the Punjab Boundary Force and asked both the dominions to assume direct control and responsibility within their respective territories. It was also agreed that both divisional headquarters be situated in Lahore (Pakistan) to ensure close co-operation, and that troops of either dominion, on guard and escort duties, would have the right of free passage across the frontier. This meeting of the Joint Defence Council was attended by Pakistan's Governor-General M.A. Jinnah; Premiers Liaquat Ali Khan, and Jawahar Lal Nehru; Field Marshal Sir Cloude Auchinleck, Supreme Commander, India and Pakistan; Lt. General Sir Rob Lockhart, Commander-in-chief, India; and Lt. General Sir Frank Messervy, Commander-in-chief, Pakistan.

Furthermore, concerted measures for the restoration of law and order and the protection of refugees both in East and West Punjab were unanimously decided at a conference held in Lahore and attended by the premiers of both the dominions, who later issued a joint statement declaring:

drastic action would be taken to put down disturbances in the Punjab; armed bands would be captured and put into concentration camps; all bands caught in the act of committing crimes would be shot on sight; both Governments would maintain the closest co-operation in ensuring the safety and security of refugees; Muslim refugee camps would be protected by Muslim troops and non-Muslim camps by non-Muslim troops, and that the refugees would be received, fed and rehabilitated in both dominions.

Over 100,000 copies of this statement in the vernacular language were dropped by Indian and Pakistani aircraft in the affected areas. A further joint statement issued by Nehru and Liaquat on 21 September declared:

Any conception of conflict between India and Pakistan is repugnant, not only on moral grounds but because any such conflict will result in disaster to both India and Pakistan. The two Governments will therefore work to the utmost of their capacity to remove causes of conflict, and to reduce as rapidly as possible both the area and intensity of the present communal conflict. In particular, statements of responsible persons which are either bellicose or one-sided will not be permitted. It is the policy of both governments to create and maintain conditions in which minorities can live in security.

These and other declarations of intent—declarations of sanity—and a series of constructive and collaborative initiatives taken by both Indian and Pakistani Governments to address jointly and separately, the grave issues of law and order and human security in the post-Partition subcontinent, generally constitute a missing link in the official and polemical histories of Partition and post-Partition eras, produced in India and Pakistan.

Also missing is the reference to the efforts of both governments—and those of the Hindu, Muslim, and Sikh volunteers—to recover hundreds and thousands of abducted women and children on both sides of the borders, and ensure their passage to safe havens. According to a report of 2 November 1947, as many as twenty-nine Muslim women were rescued from the Sikhs in East Punjab and sheltered in the Baoli camp in Lahore. These women were later returned to their relatives. Thirty-eight other women, who also arrived at the Baoli camp with the same group, were sent to Sir Ganga Ram widows' house as their relatives could not be traced. On 14 November, thirty-four abducted Muslim women and children, recovered by Indian troops, were handed over to the Pakistani Government officials in Kasur. The next day, some hundred non-Muslim women recovered by Pakistan Police, and seventy non-Muslim women recovered by Pakistani troops, were handed over to Indian officials at the non-Muslim evacuees camp at Jhang. Another report of 2 December says that fifty Muslim men, ninety-two women, and forty-six children were recovered from Amritsar, and evacuated to Pakistan; while nine non-Muslims and one abducted girl were recovered from the Lyallpur district and handed over to Indian troops in Lyallpur.

Understandably not all the volunteers, policemen, military, and others involved in the rescue and escort operations or assistance work in the camps—nor all those looking after the recovered abducted women could be described as conscientious, dedicated, noncommunal humanists. There are witnesses' accounts indicating that many of them were involved—directly or indirectly—in looting and plunder, murder, sexual savagery, and even in the abduction of women. But what is important to stress is the fact that the crimes were committed by members of all three communities—Hindus, Sikhs, and Muslims. Likewise, even in the midst of the tension, violence, and communal frenzy, many officials belonging to both governments often risked their own lives, separately and jointly, undertaking bold measures to restore law and order in the affected areas, lead the uprooted multitude to places of safety, recover abducted women and children and trace their relatives to ensure speedy reintegration of split families. This is an important aspect of the human dimension of Partition and, until very recently, was rarely, if ever, mentioned.

Memory's New Voices

A major change, however, seems to be in the offing. A more holistic and humanistic perspective is emerging and the refugee voices—especially those of women—are growing louder. The regime of silence seems to be crumbling and refugee voices and refugee memories are criss-crossing the length and breadth of India and Pakistan. These voices and memories are important, and may well play a healing role. Indeed, a number of studies on Partition released in India and Pakistan in recent years—studies giving voice to the memories of Partition refugees—strongly suggest that refugee memory may succeed in a region where numerous initiatives for healing the wounds of Partition have failed.[9] These include Urvashi Butalia's *The Other Side of Silence: Voices from the Partition of India,* and Ritu Menon and Kamla Bhasin's *Borders & Boundaries: Women in India's Partition.* These and many other studies on Partition refugees are important works. They present the complexities of Partition and project the sufferings of members of all three religious communities who suffered in the aftermath of the Partition.

Knowing more about the acts of courage and humanism engaged in by members of all three warring communities, like listening to the voices of Partition refugees, may genuinely help de-communalize images of the past and future in both India and Pakistan. To illustrate the point, one may refer here to a project on Partition—progressing under the guidance of a team of social scientists—whose objective is to prepare a new oral history of Partition by talking to several hundred survivors in India, Pakistan, and Bangladesh. 'The hope', according to project director Ashis Nandy, 'is that, as with journeys through madness, this journey of exploration may turn out to be a step towards our alternative, enriched form of sanity, provided one knows how to work through memories'.[10] Highlighting different aspects of Partition, Nandi adds that most of the survivors who were interviewed had 'at least one story to tell about how a member of the "enemy community" helped them and saved their lives'. He then quotes another survivor who said: 'People weren't evil. The times were bad.'

The current era is doubtless different from the Partition days. With the arrival of the post-Partition generations on the scene, the events and tragedies of 1947 and after, are now being viewed more dispassionately. Refugee memory no longer screams violence; it no longer reasons vendetta. More and more decommunalized, it whispers sadness, remorse, and guilt. It now talks of the good old days as well. Of course, the expressed desire is not to dismantle the borders. The borders may stay, but imposed and irrational enmity needs to go. At a popular level—in India as well as in Pakistan—there is a stronger urge today to turn away from a past which suddenly began fomenting hatred and spitting fire. Now the quest is for the other past—a past which was real, more harmonious, and which is no more. On both sides of the borders, the quest is to discover this past by rediscovering the culture of peace in the subcontinent.[11] A more dispassionate and de-communalized refugee memory may clearly assist the quest for this forbidden past, and may eventually help to heal the wounds of Partition.

Notes

1. Ranabir Samaddar, 'The History that Partition Creates', in Ranabir Samaddar (ed.), *Reflections on Partition in the East* (New Delhi: Vikas Publishing House, 1997), p. 3.

2. Ian Talbot, 'Literature and the Human Drama of the 1947 Partition', in Ian Talbot and Gurharpal Singh (eds), *Region & Partition, Bengal, Punjab and the Partition of the Subcontinent* (Karachi: Oxford University Press, 1999), pp. 228–52.

3. Ian Talbot, *Freedom's Cry: The Popular Dimension in the Pakistan Movement and Partition Experience in North-West India* (Oxford: Oxford University Press, 1996), p. 157.

4. Shahidi Jathas were *armed* Sikh groups formed to safeguard Sikh religious places and properties and protect the Sikh community during Partition disturbances. But the Shahidi Jathas also went on the offensive and attacked Muslims in different areas of the Punjab.

5. Andrew Whitehead, 'Women Victims of Partition—Brutalised and Humiliated', *The Indian Express*, 1 August 1997.

6. M.S. Randhawa, *Out of the Ashes* (Jullundhar, 1954), p. 27.

7. K.S. Duggal, *Twice-Born Twice-Dead*, translated by J. Ara (New Delhi: Vikas, 1979), pp. 136–7. The term *charpoy* means light bed; *Kirpan* is a long knife, a weapon generally kept by Sikhs; *Jalebi* is a sweet.

8. Romila Thapar, *The Post and Prejudice* (New Delhi: National Book Trust, 1975), p. 1.

9. *See*, in this regard, Maren and Marcelo Viñar's article, 'Terrorisme d'Etat et subjectivité' in *Transeuropéennes*, n° 18.

10. 'Old Journeys Revisited', in *Economist*, 12 February 2000.

11. *See* Syed Sikander Mehdi, 'Rediscovering the Culture of Peace in South Asia', in *Henderik Bullens*, Sciitsu Tachibana and Wayne Reynolds (eds), *Restructuring Security Concepts, Postures and Industrial Base* (Mobach: AFES Press, 1997), pp. 187–97.

Families, Displacement

MEGHNA GUHATHAKURTA

Until recently, apart from a few historical accounts, writings about the partition of the subcontinent have mainly been centred around fictional literature and autobiographical writings. The tendency has been to focus on the communal and violent nature of the Partition and the mass exodus accompanying it, whereas forced migration actually took place more along the Punjab frontier. Along the Bengal border the situation was different. For some families it was a matter of conscious choice; for example, families whose members were in government service were given an option to take equivalent work on the other side. Some families, however, had to decide very quickly, and later perhaps regretted their decision. For others, the decision to migrate was taken almost overnight, especially if the family was directly or indirectly hit by anyone of the communal uprisings which succeeded the Partition. But, for most families, the decision to migrate was deliberated slowly, and in waves, within the circles of the family—a process which continues even today. This had a curious effect on the social makeup of the region resulting in a Diaspora of families; Hindus, Muslims, Biharis, Chakmas, Garos and so on. were separated and divided, taking up life on either side of the lines chalked out by the Radcliffe Award,[1] each group engrossed in its own struggle for survival or achievement, yet still connected to the others by emotional, imaginary, and real ties.

Fear, Memory, and the Context

This is not to say that the Bengal Partition occurred without violence or was not stricken by communal forces. Violence is not always to be measured by outward acts of murder, looting, or abduction. And while reports suggest that the intensity of such acts in pre- and post-Partition Bengal was as great as in the Punjab, their occurrence may have been more sporadic. Violence typifies a state where a sense of fear is generated and perpetrated in such a way as to make it systemic, pervasive, and inevitable. Thus, during the nine-month occupation of Dhaka by the Pakistani army in 1971—in what General Yahya Khan referred to as a 'normal and peaceful' situation—people went about their daily chores in dread and fear, not knowing when a tap on the door could mean death or (for women) rape. In the many communal riots which both preceded and followed the Partition, it was the fear of being persecuted, dispossessed, not belonging, rather than actual incidents of violence, that caused many to flee. In many cases this fear was deliberately generated, for example by leaflets or newspaper reports, the sources often being rumours or the mere example of seeing your neighbours leave. In interviewing migrants across the borders, one is astounded by the number of people who say they did not actually witness any act of violence, but fled because they had heard a mob was coming their way, or that the next village was ablaze or even by idle chatter which led them to believe that the country no longer belonged to them. Nor do actual incidents of violence always cause people to flee; there are always those who, given the choice, will choose to remain. Fear is less derived from actual acts of violence than it is from perceptions of violence. People resist migration for many reasons, and nowhere are those reasons more rich or varied than in the case of the Bengal Partition.

The Porous Border between the Two Bengals

The two Bengals enjoyed open borders for a long period of time: it was not until 1953 that passports were introduced, and only after the 1965 Indo-Pakistan War were visas required. Rail and air communication stopped after the 1965 war, and only very restrictive overland links were maintained. But people on both sides of the border, both for trading as well as other social reasons, defied these restrictions persistently, so much so that a whole network of underground operators, who helped people cross borders without visas or passports—a method often colourfully termed in the local language as 'gola-dhakka' passage (taking you by the scruff of your neck and pushing you across) grew steadily. The Bangladesh Liberation War in 1971 and the resulting mass exodus of people fleeing persecution, threw these borderlines and boundaries into question. Despite this porosity, 'illegal' trade or smuggling has been a primary concern for successive national governments and 'border incidents' or skirmishes between border forces have captured front-page news. This phenomenon has reached its peak now that both Hindu and Muslim economic migrants are crossing frontiers by the thousands in search of better means of livelihood.

As far as Partition is concerned, there has been a further silencing process at work in the writings about the two Bengals. Although fiction and autobiographical writings have dominated the Partition discourse, the voices of Hindu migrants from East Bengal have been more prominent than those of Muslim migrants from West Bengal. The reason for this is, of course, an open question which awaits further research. But one of the important distinctions between the two 'migrant' groups has been brought on by the political conditions of the country they migrated to: for Hindus, the experience has been primarily one of dispossession and nostalgia for their 'homesteads' (*Bhitabari*)—something very pronounced and glorified in their writings. For many Muslims of a particular generation, the journey to Pakistan was like travelling to a 'promised land'—an image which later became tarnished as Pakistan entered its most repressive stage under the Ayub regime, with the brunt of it being borne by the people of East Bengal. In the oppressive atmosphere of a martial-law regime, whose favourite occupation was 'India-bashing', it was understandably very difficult to write, much less be nostalgic about one's homeland in India. There is a reticence, even now, among Bengali Muslims to talk publicly of their '*desh*' (the term for 'ancestral home' in the Bengali language) if it happens to be in India. Recording family histories, however, makes it to some extent possible to overcome this barrier: they provide a space for talking freely about nostalgic memories of childhood, growing up, family ties and accompanying emotions without the direct intrusion of nationalist politics.

Another phenomenon distinguishes East Bengali reminiscences of the Partition from those in West Bengal: the Bangladesh Liberation War of 1971. Memories of 1947, or Partition, have often been superseded by memories of 1971 (or the movements leading up to 1971), because in the quest for a Bengali identity many Bengali Muslims have had to rethink their positions. As memories of the Partition are revived, they are often either blocked or coloured by memories of 1971. Many Muslims came to the East from West Bengal and Bihar in the hope of finding their promised land—not all of whom necessarily believed in the Muslim League ideology.[2] Many progressive cultural activists and professionals came from Calcutta, not spontaneously, but nevertheless with the ambition of constructing a new nation that would give shape and colour to their dreams. But for most this dream was short-lived. The repression of a Bengali identity and the imposition of a new Pakistani cultural identity and martial law brought about spontaneous resistance from the people, whether in the form of the 1952 Language Movement, or the anti-Ayub demonstrations in 1969, culminating in the 1971 Liberation War for an independent Bangladesh. But, whereas in the nationalist writing of history these events appear in a linear schema, the personal histories of those involved in or affected by them were far from linear. Rather, these events foregrounded the contradictions of identity which the individuals concerned had to confront in their personal lives as they contested the different notions of nationhood in the political arena: one based on the Bengali language and the other on Islam. This is why—even in present day Bangladesh—narratives of the Liberation War are still a site for contestation between rival Bengali and Bangladeshi nationalism.

From Family Narratives to Social History

Dominant historiographical trends construe the 1947 Partition of the subcontinent as a product of the colonial state, as well as a landmark in the progressive march towards achieving modern nationhood. In subsequent years, this nationhood came to determine questions of citizenship and social exchange, while also defining personal identities for the people occupying the new territories of India and Pakistan. One of the main critiques of this view had come from the subaltern school which maintains that there exist groups like peasants, women, and others whose voices have remained silent or marginalized, and who may possess a notion of community different from—or even in opposition to—that of the nationalist project.

My focus on family histories uses the above perspective both as a starting point and a springboard from which to explore the problematics of looking at the social history of a people who have been disempowered by developments beyond their control but who, at the same time, have sought to retain an element of control in their attempts to adapt to the new situation. Family histories provide us with a conceptual tool through which such processes can be better understood. Looking at family histories enables us to (a) look at Partition from a site that is intermediate to—but not wholly exclusive from—larger structural forces on the one hand and individual decision-making on the other and (b) to locate Partition and what it represents on the temporal scale of generations, because family histories are about inter-generational exchanges. To focus on the family as an important intermediary site, therefore, is to see how memories of individuals and generations are constructed and negotiated; how personal identities of gender, class, or nation are formed, conformed to, contested, and confronted.

Feminist scholarship helps us to comprehend families as a site where identities of gender, community, class, and religion are intertwined, generating a politics that is gendered—whether along class, religious, or national lines. Feminist rethinking of the family has important implications for the study of Partition because it has foregrounded a number of questions: the myth of the monolithic family, with the husband in the role of breadwinner as the only legitimate form, has been challenged; feminists have reclaimed the family for social and historical analysis breaking it down into underlying structures of sex, gender, and generation; because families are structured around gender and age, women, men, boys, and girls do not experience their families in the same way, and feminists have explored the differentiation of the family experience mystified by the glorification of motherhood, love, and the images of the family as a domestic haven. Feminists have also raised questions about the illusory nature of the isolation of the nuclear family, arguing there are close connections between the internal lives of families and the organization of the economy, the state, and other institutions. A distinction must be made here between families and households. Households are the empirical measurable units within which people pool resources and perform certain tasks. Families on the other hand can be identified at two levels: as normative constructs based on conjugality; or as a more extended network of kin relations that people may activate selectively. In this sense, the family depicts an ideological construct whereby people get recruited into households. It is through an active process of selection (who is family and who is not) that people experience the absence or presence, the sharing or withholding, of basic poolable resources.

This distinction is particularly useful in the context of the Bengal Partition, where families may be dislocated, but where certain functions of resource pooling (both material and ideological) by various members may determine their recruitment into the family. In Bangla, for example, the semantics of the term family differs and in the empirical context may have multiple connotations. Family, as the ideal patrilineal conjugal family, is called *Poribar*; relatives and kinfolk, inclusive of those of patrilineal descent, but embracing distant relatives (paternal and maternal), is called *Atyio*—or, as a clustered group. *Atyio-shojon* (kinfolk). Thus, if family is looked upon as an ideology and an extended network of kin relations that may be activated selectively, applying it to families divided by the Partition generates some interesting data regarding the boundaries of who constitutes family: who is in the category of *atyio* (relatives), who is family at one level (e.g., through resource distribution), or who is only symbolically part of the family even though they may be blood relatives.

Two Family Histories

I have studied two families: one Muslim from Barasat, West Bengal; the other Hindu from Barisal, East Bengal—the latter being my own family (though it is my aunt—herself a witness to Partition—rather than myself who is the prime narrator). In both cases, the interviewees are men and women who have crossed the borders, whether in 1947 or afterwards. as a result of the aftermath of Partition.

The structures of the two families are different: the family from Barasat was land-centred, hence patrilineal and location-specific. The family from Banaripara was not dependent on land, but rather capitalized on education and the service sector. However, many of the marriage alliances which took place were with the landed gentry—and these alliances were used for resource pooling within the family.

In the first instance, almost everyone married into the same district or at least neighbouring ones, whether they happened to be settled in West or East Bengal. The residences of the family were thus both location-specific and patrilineal. Apart from the families who migrated to Bangladesh, and one member of the Barasat family who settled in another village in West Bengal, most of the family members still live in the natal village—though they have separate households. In the second instance, marriages took place with families in other districts, essentially within East Bengal. Because the members of the family were not directly dependent on land, and the ancestral home existed mostly at a symbolical level, the residence pattern was scattered. A general pattern emerged where the tendency was to move towards the urban centres: Mymensingh, Dhaka, and above all Calcutta. Though due to dependence on white-collar jobs, the gravitation towards the metropolis was not always through patrilineal connections, but was often the result of connections through marriage. Thus, many cousins in the Hindu family grew up in their *Mamabari* or maternal uncle's house. All this was a pre-Partition syndrome. When the Partition occurred, this was the context in which family members made their own decisions.

Calcutta was the metropolis of British India, and as such the focal point of migration. Urban migration had been increasing since the forties, especially during and after the famine of 1943. The family from Barasat, though land-centred, was also living in the vicinity of Calcutta. This determined their mind-set when the decision to move or not was thrown open to them. Both property-related concerns and the desire to live in the vicinity of Calcutta—with educational and employment opportunities for children—became important considerations to affect their attitude, and East Bengal or Pakistan came to be seen as more 'backward'. It is interesting to note that many Muslim middle-class families of both East and West Bengal villages returned to Pakistan after the Partition. But artists, writers, journalists, and other professionals of West-Bengali origin came, bringing with them their, talents and skill. Later they not only made names for themselves, but contributed to the movement for a 'Bengali identity' in the state of Pakistan.

Hindu service workers had started their migratory trend towards Calcutta long before everyone else, for reasons of education and employment. But Dhaka and Mymensingh were also important urban centres. This pre-partition migration, like any other urban migratory trend, used family connections and contacts to establish a 'chain' which enabled other family members to follow. When Partition came, this 'chain' was stretched to its limits and often broke. At this juncture, migrants became refugees.

New   Interpretations

My particular methodological intervention was aimed at revealing gendered narratives in family histories. This task was made easier since in both the families I interviewed, I found women, who, during the Partition, were unmarried and as a consequence were forced to migrate for reasons of physical security. Arjoo, from the Muslim family in West Bengal, was barely twelve when she was forced to leave her mother for the security of East Pakistan where her elder brother lived. The incident is related in her own poignant words:

Everyone got panicky. I remember some outsiders came and put fire to some houses in Kazipara, a nearby village. I heard the rumour and panicked. At that time my mother and I were alone in the house. I ran and hid in the sugar cane field for an hour. My mother didn't go with me. Being the youngest in the family I used to be the only one to go to the Kazipara primary school. The rest of the family had attended the village school. But after the riots my father put pressure on me to go and stay in East Pakistan with my brother. Both I and my mother resisted at first, but my father said he would stop my education if I didn't listen to him. My mother then laid out the options to me and said that either I go or my education will be stopped. I was determined to get an education. So I went. I remember before I left a goat was sacrificed on my behalf.

About community relations, she tells the following story:

I have fond memories of my school at Kazipara. I still maintain contact with some of my friends. I had mostly Hindu friends. I remember no signs of discrimination but there were differences. For example I remember we had a crazy teacher called Ganesh. Hindu girls used to say '*aggey*' in answering to roll call and Muslim girls used to say '*ji*'. Once my Hindu friend said '*ji*' instead and immediately Ganesh sir reacted. You are a Hindu he said why should you say '*ji*'!

Arjoo's perception of nation or homeland was mediated through kinship and marital relations: she married someone whose ancestral home was in Jessore, which meant double dislocation for her. Not only did she feel herself to be an outsider in East Pakistan or Bangladesh, she was also an outsider in her in-law's house. She relates her experience as a new bride: 'I felt the differences of being from West Bengal although I was not openly told it.' She said there was differences in their dialect and hers. Her in-laws used to tease her and called her '*khuni*' (murderer) because she spoke in her local dialect '*jabokhuni kabhokhuni*' instead of '*jaboney khaboney*'. Sometimes she could not understand her mother-in-law when she asked her to come down from the roof (*ulla aia*), because Ulla was the name of her village.

Arjoo feels proud of her natal village in Barasat. She visits it often, but sometimes has to fight with her husband for that right. When her husband asks her why she goes there so often, saying there is no need to go there now that she is married, she replies that as long as she has strength she will go. 'Once I lose my strength I will automatically stop'. She visits with her children—a boy and two girls. Once when she took her son there he was surprised when he got down at Barasat and remarked: 'Mom! But we have only come to Jessore!'

Tapati, from the Hindu family in East Bengal, was more insecure in her perceptions of family, community, and homeland/nation, perhaps due to the very disturbing and traumatic experiences of her adolescence and adult life. Tapati's miseries did not stop with the Partition. In 1957, she married and began living in a joint family, which soon broke up. 1971 brought the tragic news about Jyotirmoy's death at the hands of the Pakistan Army. Most tragic of all was when, in 1980, her husband died of a heart attack leaving her to fend for herself and two unmarried daughters. Incidents like these make her equate home with homeland in terms of it being a source of constant insecurity. In her own words: 'I could never find stability. I lost my father when I was only a few months old. Throughout my life I have been compelled to leave one home for another. Even now that is my reality.' Tapati has no nostalgia about her homeland, only memories, which she never glorifies. Her life has been too unsettling and she still relives the trauma in her everyday life. She is afraid whenever she reads in the papers about the Tenancy Act being revoked, withdrawing the rights of the tenant; she quakes with fear that the house she is living in might suddenly collapse because it is built on uncertain foundations. Her only concern is for the security of her daughters and herself.

Family histories of the Partition therefore make a strong statement about social transformation. They reiterate that families are open to the winds of change, changing themselves and thereby changing social reality. Times of transition are trying times when such changes may come about quite suddenly creating havoc and upheaval that haunts one into the next century. Hopefully further research into this area will reveal to us some of the answers to questions which have been long haunting us in our own histories.

Notes

1. Two Boundary Commissions were set up by the British Administration on 30 June 1947 to draw up the frontiers of India and Pakistan. Sir Cyril Radcliffe was named Chairperson of both the Commissions, one to determine the Punjab frontier, the other to determine the Bengal frontier, inclusive of the Sylhet and Assam border. The four-person commission consisted of four High Court judges, two nominated by the Congress Party and two by the Muslim League. The commissioners were to demarcate boundaries on the basis of ascertaining the contiguous majority areas of Muslims and non-Muslims. In the actual deliberations, it was found that both in the Punjab and in Bengal, the divergence of opinion was so wide that they could not come to an agreed solution Therefore on the strength of his casting vote, each of the awards was virtually the decision of Commission Chairman Sir Radcliffe. For a detailed analysis of the period of dissection see. H.V. Hodson. *The Great Divide: Britain–India–Pakistan*, (London: Hutchinson and Co. Ltd.; Karachi: Oxford University Press, Karachi. 1969)

2. The Muslim League in Bengal was formed in May 1936 at the initiative of

Nawab Habibulla of Dhaka, as a new party to represent the Muslims. Styling itself as the United Muslim Party, it was set up to take the place of the provincial Muslim League which had fallen into decay. The new party was in fact an electoral alliance between several of the most prominent and powerful Muslim families of Bengal. The Muslim League ideology first of all appealed to the simple notion of Muslim unity and the welfare of the Muslim community as a whole. By 1940, however, the All India Muslim League was orchestrating the demand for independent Muslim states in north-western and north-eastern India.

References

Nari: Protinidhitta O Rajniti. Women: Representation and Politics (dir.), Dhaka: Centre for Social Studies, 1997.

Comparative Feminist Perspectives (dir.), Dhaka: UPL, 1997.

Living on the Edge: Essays on the Chittagong Hill Tracts (dir.), Kathmandu: SAFHR, 1997.

SAARC *Beyond State Centric Cooperation* (dir.), Dhaka: Centre for Social Studies, 1992.

The Politics of British Aid Policy Formation the Case of British Aid to Bangladesh, 1972–1986, Dhaka: Centre for Social Studies, 1990.

Nari Rastro Motadorsho Women, State and Ideology (dir.), Dhaka: Centre for Social Studies, 1990.

The Mostar Story,
or the Twenty-first-century Berlin*

OZREN KEBO

Mostar was a city of one hundred thousand before the war. Spreading out over both banks of the Neretva, it was one of the few cities in the world to have the canyon of a river running through it. Formerly the political, administrative, cultural, and economic centre of Herzegovina, Mostar today is a town demolished, bloodstained, and split, unable to even be its own centre.

For civilized countries and civilized people, Einstein is enough. We needed Karadžić, Boban, Tudjman, and Milošević to understand that everything is relative. Let me explain indirectly: 1992 is considered to have been the hardest in Sarajevo's long history. I felt part of the hardship on my own skin. I live in the quarter that Serbian artillery was especially fond of. Between eight and nine one morning, the children in my skyscraper counted some 470 grenades fall in the range of 200 metres around the building. We thought that was the worst hell a man could get into.

But, as I said, everything is relative. A man who had been with us in 1992, spent all of 1993 in Mostar, a town 130 kilometres south-west of Sarajevo. When he returned in 1994, he told us that we knew nothing about shelling. Because we hadn't been in Mostar. What he had survived there can be compared to nothing else. From the Croatian western part of the town, carpets of grenades fell incessantly on the east (Bosnian) side. 'Carpet' is the colloquial term used in Bosnia for continuous shelling, that goes on endlessly

* Translated from the Bosnian by Teodora Tabacki

evenly covering the entire town. Persian carpets are considered the best in the world, with vivid colours, plentiful knitting, and an immense number of knots per square meter. Among the worst are those of Mostar, with thousands of grenades fired per hour on one square kilometre.

So much for the theory of relativity. And now a few words on the consequences. When he visited Mostar after the war, Sarajevan writer Alija Isakovic called it hell gone cold. It was a moving sight. The Croatian half of the town was almost undamaged. The Bosnian side ... totally demolished. All, absolutely all, its buildings were destroyed. Houses, monuments, mosques, churches, parks, streets. Can you imagine a town—half a town, that is—with not one glass, not one window saved! That is the story of Mostar in 1994. Through the centre of the town, two hundred meters west of the Neretva river, runs the Boulevard. A light railroad used to run there. Later, a four-lane road was put through and named the Boulevard. This romantically named roadway still divides the town in half, where one part was pretty much destroyed, then mostly repaired, but left absolutely frustrated, while the other was preserved in term of its construction but left full of hatred—that is, emotionally demolished.

The War in Mostar: Basic Facts

And now some basic data on the war itself. The attacks on Mostar had already begun by the autumn of 1991. Reserve corps from the Yugoslav National Army (YNA), brought in from Montenegro, started to bully the inhabitants as soon as they arrived. All those incidents indicated that war was ahead. People expected it to happen, but no one could imagine the damage it would do to the town. Montenegrin reservists did not limit themselves to mere provocation—drinking in town bars until late in the night, then partying in the streets, shooting, causing street fights, and provoking the locals. One of the reservists did what no one had ever done before. He got drunk, got behind the wheel of a military transport truck, and drove across Mostar's icon, the Old Bridge, a pearl of world architecture. The Old Bridge had been built in 1566. Not even a motorcycle had ever crossed it, not to mention a transport vehicle. It was seen as one of most impressive symbols of Bosnia and Herzegovina.

War started soon thereafter. It was a heavy, devastating conflict. Mostar had seven bridges. The YNA forces destroyed six. Only the most beautiful was left—the old bridge. Somewhat damaged by detonations and a few grenades, it still bridged the waters of the Neretva intact. A joint effort of Croatian and Bosnian forces ousted the YNA from Mostar. Then the Croatian forces attacked the town on the 9 May 1993 with the idea of turning it into a national Croatian capital and integrating it into Croatia. That is how the worst period in the town's history—and one of the darkest European adventures in the second half of the twentieth century—began.

The Dark Side of Man

There is written evidence of criminal intent. The Government of Herzeg-Bosnia and the Croatian Defence Corps (CDC) have, in their constitutional documents clearly stated their authority over ethnically pure space. What was announced theoretically in those documents, was brought about through genocide.

Concentration camps were soon established for Bosnians. All men apt for military service, found in the part of town under CDC control, were interned. Thousands of men and women passed through the camps in the beginning. I know of an old woman of eighty who was stripped naked, humiliated, robbed of all her money and jewellery, and finally expelled to the 'Muslim half of the town'. In those first days of war, several thousand Bosnians were gathered in the football stadium under Bijeli Breg. Footage of that incredible scene was seen around the world, as the Bosnians were transferred from there directly to concentration camps, where they were savagely tortured. People were beaten to death. Sadism lasted for hours.

As meals in the camp, Bosnians were given hot liquid, which looked and poured more like water than porridge or soup. It was hot, extremely hot, and the prisoners were given two minutes to eat it. If someone overstepped the allowed two-minute limit, his 'lunch' was taken away and he was beaten. So how do you eat something that burns your stomach in two minutes? A solution was found: in the trenches around the bunkhouses, the prisoners found old plastic Coca-Cola bottles. Dirty but useable. In the evening, they would urinate in them and then in the morning use their cold urine to cool the hot 'porridge'. And ate it like that. There were people who only came to the camp to beat the prisoners. One prisoner was beaten and then taken to the other prisoners with a 700 DM ransom on his head. That was the price the torturers wanted for sparing his life. The prisoners collected the money, sacrificing for a friend their last marks used for bribing the guards and buying short-term mercy. They saved the man, but for a long time couldn't look at him, as he had been totally deformed by the beating.

In the town the situation is similar. The CDC was set on implementing the concept of an exclusively Croatian area. Women were raped, the elderly expelled to the left bank. It happened more than once that a married couple was taken away in the middle of the night, thrown out of their apartment and sent across the Boulevard in the morning. When they reached the halfway point, they were shot in the back. For days, weeks, even months no one was allowed to remove the bodies. Anyone who tried to approach them was shot at. To give just a single example: that is how the beloved professor Semsudin Serdarevic and his wife Remza were killed. For weeks their bodies were left to rot on the boulevard. In the end, they were eaten by hungry stray dogs. Their two sons now live in Norway and suffer at the mere thought of Mostar.

There are thousands of similar stories. All share a common characteristic: both the names of victims and the names of the perpetrators are known. It is estimated that in the western part of the town some seven hundred people await indictments from The Hague.

On 9 November, the Croatian Defence Corps did something unthinkable: early in the morning, the Old Bridge was pulled down. A few grenades were all that was needed to bring the five hundred year-old edifice crashing into the Neretva with a heavy and painful roar. A painful, incredibly painful moment. People from the left bank forgot about the grenades, emerged from their basements and stared in disbelief at the hole where the Bridge had stood. On the right side they were savagely celebrating, firing in the air with their Kalashnikovs. It was no small thing: they had torn down the greatest symbol of Islamic culture. And thereby completed a complicated task: they had already destroyed all the mosques on 'their' territory.

Guilt, Collectivity, Reconciliation

I have heard hundreds of stories from that period. It is hard to conceive that man could do such things to fellow man. I shall mention only a few. Eight soldiers of the CDC battered an old woman of fifty-five to death. In fact they only thought they had battered her to death. She survived. She doesn't know how either. When they left, she crawled up to the doorway of her building, beaten, covered with blood and bruises, her clothes shredded. But none of her Croatian neighbours—fearing for their lives dared to take her in. Nor help her. She kept on crawling. It took her the whole night to get to the left bank. Or another example: a man escaped from the Heliodrom concentration camp. The CDC sent an official notice over the radio (remember that: the call was official): if he didn't surrender within 48 hours, his wife and children would be shot. When he approached houses near Mostar, to ask for or steal food, he heard the notice. He surrendered immediately. Five soldiers battered him savagely. He told them: 'You have to kill me. If you don't kill me now, a day will come when I will kill you'. He survived. One more example: two nine-year-old brothers were overheard saying: 'It is better that mum died. It is better for her. They did horrible things to her'. Their mother had first been raped on an open field and then endlessly beaten by the CDC soldiers. She ended up in hospital and died after seven days.

And so on. Going on with such stories would take days. Mostar lives with them. The wounds are deep and are not healing.

Let us be perfectly clear: we are not dealing here with the collective guilt of a nation—Croatian in this case. Crime is always the act of an individual. Or, in the worst case, of an organized group—not of a nation. I also know of dozens of examples of Bosnian Croatians risking their lives to hide hapless Bosnians in their apartments and cupboards. Their names are also known, though it is unwise to mention them. A day will come when those people will be proud of their courage. For the time being, they are forced to hide it.

What we are talking about is a bizarre political system, designed by Franjo Tudjman, the late President of the Republic of Croatia. The division of Bosnia and Herzegovina remained his obsession until death. When he was told in 1993 by his closest associates that the members of the Croatian Defence Corps were setting up concentration camps where Bosnians were being put, tortured, and murdered, he angrily retorted: 'So what! We are at war. Everybody has concentration camps.'

Terrible things were happening. Throughout it all, a relentless media campaign was waged, whose exclusive goal was to hide and justify crimes, blame them on the other side, logistically prepare for partition. The logic was inconceivable: I am shelling you day and night, killing, torturing, wearing you down—and I'm still angry at you. Indescribably angry. At that time, the journalists engaged in this campaign were stars. They had money and every possible privilege. Now they are lonely and despised. The Croatian Democratic Community (HDZ) is not paying them salaries. Many are paranoid of being followed and hounded. Guilty conscience makes it impossible to put behind and forget what has been done.

Partition

Before the war, along with Vukovar, Mostar had the greatest number of mixed marriages. It was an example of harmonious coexistence. It was famous for its anti-fascist tradition from the Second World War. None of that helped. It even made things worse.

I just mentioned Vukovar. Vukovar and Dubrovnik in Croatia, Mostar in Bosnia and Herzegovina, had similar fates. Dubrovnik and Vukovar were destroyed by Serbian forces; Mostar by Croatian forces. All three towns are trying to get back to normal. The process is easiest in Dubrovnik, somewhat harder in Vukovar, and hardest of all—that is, it is inexistent—in Mostar. When I mention that fact to some of my Croatian friends from Mostar, they say the situations are not alike. They consider the destruction of Vukovar and Dubrovnik to be criminal and savage acts, while the destruction of Mostar is seen as the legitimate defence of Croatian national interests. That type of thinking—whereby a crime is not automatically a crime, but whose nature is determined by those who committed it—makes our situation ultimately complicated. There is no catharsis, no remorse, no denazification. No understanding of the horrors that took place. They are not even seen as horrors, but as highly moral and patriotic deeds.

Peace—a bad one, but peace nonetheless—has lasted for six years now. Things are hardly back to normal in Mostar. It is still a divided town, with a clear demarcation line running right down the Boulevard. There are people who are refugees in the eastern part of the town; who, from the windows of other people's flats, where they are temporary residents, look at their windows in the western side of the town; at their homes, to which, for long while yet, they will be unable to return. To which they may never be able to return. Political structures in the western part prohibit any sort of rapprochement. Normalization is a chimera. The gap is deepened whenever possible.

Steps forward are small and insignificant. Spokesmen of the idea of a unified, multi-ethnic town find comfort in the following logic: it is impossible that a town remain divided; it is inconceivable that it belong to a single nation alone; there is no logic in perpetuating this situation; it is against God and common sense that crimes be left unpunished. But the situation goes on. With no end in sight.

Lies of the Island: Cyprus[*]

AHMET ALTAN

[...] The smell of war, like the smell of something burning, comes from far away. On the television, we see the Prime Minister, the Foreign Minister, the Commander of the Turkish Forces in Cyprus, the MHP youth, Denktash, and the journalists.

As you look at them, don't you wonder where the Turkish Cypriots are?

Did you ever—either in a newspaper or on a TV screen—come across any of the representatives of the Turkish-Cypriot political parties represented in parliament?

Don't you consider the absence of the Turkish Cypriot politicians strange, when on a very serious issue, from which even war could erupt, all you hear are statements from Turkish politicians and their collaborator, Denktash?

Don't you find this absence rather odd?

No, you don't, because you do not notice that there are Turkish Cypriots living in Cyprus. You almost did not even notice their representatives; you do not know what they think. Turkish Cypriots' views and thoughts are not reflected in the Turkish press or on television. They are forbidden by an unnamed law.

In order not to have any insight into our Cyprus policy, which is entirely based on lies, the opposition parties in Cyprus have been continuously subjected to censorship in Turkey,

* Writer and democracy-activist Ahmed Altan wrote this text during the escalating tension between Turkey and Greece around the issue of Cyprus in the summer of 1996. This short extract stands as a testimony, bearing witness, in a moment of threat, in a place weakened by censorship. An expanded version of this text was published under the same title in Yeni Yuzyit on 20 August 1996.

I served as a soldier for one year in a border battalion in Cyprus, I have some information about what is going on there. Turkish Cypriots and Turks from Turkey do not like each other much. If you enter a shop in a military uniform, you will be received coldly. Most Turkish Cypriots want our soldiers withdrawn.

If they come to trust you (the Turkish Cypriots), they will tell you the following: 'Robbing and killing people was unknown to us. We have learned it since the Turks arrived.' Mainland Turks continuously disgrace the Turkish Cypriots by telling them 'we have liberated you' and boasting about it.

These are 'emotional' interactions between Turkish Cypriots and mainland Turks. There are, however, more concrete facts.

The per capita income on the Greek Cypriot side is US$18,000. In comparison, the per capita income on the Turkish side is US$2500. Inflation on the Turkish side is uncontrolled, production is at a standstill, and there are no investments. It has been turned into one of the most important centres of narcotics smuggling in the world. Names of top people in Cyprus are said to be involved. There are Turkish parliamentarians who were caught while engaging in smuggling.

There are 35,000 civil servants in the TRNC which has a total population of 170,000, and their salary is sent over from Turkey. Many of the Turkish Cypriots want to get rid of Turkey. On the other hand, we are trying to 'liberate' them by force. As it was clearly put by former Turkish Foreign Minister Mumtaz Soysal: 'Even if the Turkish Cypriots do not want it, we want to liberate them'.

Exactly what the British said about India, Soysal is saying of the Cypriots.

Moreover, it is not clear what kind of benefits are provided for Turkey by keeping part of Cyprus in its hands. We are continuously sending money to Cyprus from Turkey. We have no economic interest there. Since we keep an army corps in Cyprus, Greece has increased its military presence on the island. If we look at it from the military point of view, we have made our rival in the Aegean bring its military power to our southern borders.

From the diplomatic point of view, the Cyprus problem has completely isolated Turkey from the world. If you look into this picture you will see a blurred image.

The Turkish Cypriots do not want to be liberated and we are trying to 'liberate' them by force. However, this liberation has no benefit for us either.

Why, then, are we doing this, being as it neither serves the Turkish people nor the Turkish Cypriots? Whom does it serve?

To answer this question you will have to ask further questions: that is, who owns the houses built by co-operatives in Cyprus? Who plundered the properties left by Greek Cypriots? Which is the other arm in Turkey of the narcotics smuggling ring in Cyprus?

Perhaps war will break out in Cyprus: perhaps people will die. You should at least know for what and for whom this war will be fought.

The Dynamics of Division

RITU MENON

In July 2000, a little over fifty years after the Partition of India, the following reports appeared in *The Times of India* on the same day. Both reported a recent visit to Pakistan by a group of Indian journalists; the first, by senior editor Dileep Padgaonkar, was entitled 'When Hatred Feeds on Hate'; the second, by freelance journalist, Sumita Mehta, was called 'People Like Us, Divided by *Hukumat*'. I quote passages from both. First, Padgaonkar:

Seen through the prism of Pakistan, India is a country that few Indians would recognise. Even sophisticated Pakistanis are convinced that India is as obsessed with Pakistan as Pakistan is with India. There is also a widespread feeling in this country that Pakistan can bleed India in Kashmir and thus retard its economic progress. Some go very much further. India's problems in the north-east, its caste wars and communal tensions, its prickly relations with other neighbours, taken together, give them the impression that it is only a matter of time before the country implodes ...

You try to explain to Pakistanis that, barring Indians of a certain age who were still nostalgic about their roots in Sialkot or Peshawar or Lahore, the rest of India isn't interested in Pakistan ...

You tell the Pakistanis that the perceptions of both India and Pakistan have been largely shaped by Punjabi media persons in both countries. It is vital to get perceptions from people from other provinces too. Moreover, it is journalists who have experienced Partition who have called the shots in the media so far. It is time to listen to the younger generation. The young, with no chip on the shoulder, might have another unsuspected story to tell.

These arguments do not sound too persuasive to them. The reason, one suspects, is that what Pakistanis dread more than Indian hostility is Indian indifference towards their country. indifference would remove the only point of reference they have to justify their often anguished search to seek parity with India, always.

And this is what Mehta has to say:

The taxi driver who takes us to Rawalpindi wants democracy but admits, at the same time, that the present regime is better than the last 'All politicians are corrupt. The last lot took money—one doesn't mind that—but they did nothing. At least, this lot is doing something,' he says. Rawalpindi is textbook Pakistan—hawkers, narrow lanes, colour and local flavour. It was a back-to-roots exercise sans escorts. Yet, at no time was there even a sense of hostility towards a woman who was clearly an Indian. Instead, a lot of warmth and fellow feeling.

'It's not you and me,' insists the old man in Lahore's Anarkali Bazar. He hands over a bottle of Bisleri. 'We have no quarrel with each other. It's the governments that perpetuate this divide. Please carry our message of peace to your *hukumat*.'

General Musharraf notwithstanding, I will.

These two reports, and others that appeared on subsequent days are, in a way, responsible for this reflection. For the past ten to fifteen years, I have been trying to understand the Partition of India at various levels: as one whose family was affected by it; as someone who has written about it from a gender perspective; as a feminist, active in the women's movement in India, and in cross-border attempts to transcend the mutual hostility between the two countries by focusing on issues of common concern; as a researcher trying to unravel the complex and increasingly troubled relationship between India and Pakistan and Bangladesh; and lastly, as a resident of a subcontinent where questions of identity, nationality, community, and gender are almost daily being redefined. Although the partition of India is no longer a 'current' conflict, so to speak, the processes that were set in motion at the time of the Independence Movement are still alive. This is especially true of identity processes which are reconfigured in response to contemporary political changes, both within our countries and between them. Other studies of the lingering impact of historical partitions—in Ireland, Israel/ Palestine, Yugoslavia, for example—grapple with similar issues, and the account which follows is indebted to them in many ways. It is also unabashedly autobiographical, drawing on my own multiple identities and involvements for its narrative.

I am Indian, a woman from erstwhile West Punjab, now in Pakistan, for whom the Indian Partition was the stuff of family history and mythology, and historical 'fact'. After 1947, no one from my family ever went back to Pakistan. Although Lahore was remembered nostalgically and lovingly, even as children we could sense an implacable antipathy developing towards 'Muslims'. This was never expressed at an individual level—how could it be?

We had so many dear friends—but directed towards them as a 'community', with all the dangerous misperceptions attendant upon this. Yet, as often happens with such contradictions this, too, remained benign. As I learnt to recognize much later, it is only in moments of stress or obvious conflict that it can become antagonistic.

I was the only member of my family to visit Pakistan, for the first time in 1987, forty years after Partition, and three years after the horrifying anti-Sikh riots in north India following Mrs. Gandhi's assassination, which propelled me into undertaking an oral history of women's experiences of Partition. My immediate family was surprised. My daughter, aged thirteen, wanted to know why I was going to an 'enemy' country. My mother-in-law didn't like the idea one bit. My mother said it was a good thing my grandmother wasn't alive, or she might have felt personally betrayed by such an obvious gesture of 'disloyalty' on my part. A couple of my uncles were amused and one aunt, frankly curious, but the rest of the family could not quite understand why I was doing what I was doing—it was a closed chapter.

But was it really? Can Pakistan ever be, for India? India, for Pakistan?

Two Solitudes

'As far as school texts are concerned', the educationist Krishna Kumar said to me, 'the latest news in modern Indian history is 1947. There's nothing after that.' He was discussing his work on the representation of the Independence Movement in Pakistani and Indian history textbooks. I have thought about what he said since, and wondered whether it is only in textbooks that the clock has stopped at 1947 for us in India—as far as Pakistan is concerned, that is. Despite what Dileep Padgaonkar says about Indian disinterest or indifference, most Indians have found it difficult to come to terms with the division of the country on the basis of religious identity. Even while we accept that self-determination may be a legitimate aspiration, the circumstances of the Indian Partition are unsettling. Perhaps this is one reason why Indian historiography of the Partition is obsessed with whys and wherefores, combing through records and documents and resolutions; discussing political developments and colonial compulsions threadbare, and endlessly debating the 'what ifs' of history in order to arrive at a reasonably acceptable explanation for what happened. Somehow, it has always seemed to me that, underlying these attempts, is a lingering regret: it needn't have happened. And so, although both countries experienced the violent and numbing consequences of division, have since been at war with each other and, in Pakistan's case, seen a new division with the emergence of Bangladesh, the creation of Pakistan in 1947 was for many Pakistanis the glorious culmination of a quest for independence not only from the British, but from 'Hindu' India. What is foregrounded is the celebration of creation rather than the piercing regret of division. This is not to say that at the individual and popular levels there was a wholesale endorsement of division; merely that, as in India, a contrary position was not expressed publicly. Clearly then, their account of the Independence Movement in history books will not be the same as ours. Obvious, but perhaps not fully internalized by us. And so we look for perfidy. For further proof of mal-intent. At the height of our paranoia we say Pakistan will not rest till it has dismembered us completely. At the height of theirs, they say India will not rest till it swallows up Pakistan, reverses the Partition. They blame India for Bangladesh, we blame them for Kashmir. They raise the bogey of RAW whenever Sind erupts, we produce the 1511 when Punjab does. Neither can forget what it believes the other has done.

And so, borders are sealed, visas are withheld, those who travel to either country must report to the police within twenty-four hours of their arrival. You can only visit the places stamped on your visa, and cantonments and border areas are out of bounds. Pakistanis must obtain a No Objection Certificate to visit India if they work for the government, Indian hosts must get the clearance of the home and external affairs ministry if they invite a Pakistani for a conference. There is no trade between the two countries, very little movement of books or periodicals, no cultural exchanges to speak of, and no cessation of hostilities for long enough to allow the healing process of normalization to take place.

There is no real conversation.

Stories of Partition and Divided Families

In 1987, I met my aunt who lives in Karachi, for the first time. She had married a Muslim before Partition, converted, changed her name, and worked as a journalist with the *Dawn* till she retired in her seventies. I had written to her to say that I was planning to interview women on their experience of Partition in India, and wanted to speak to her, too, about it. Perhaps because she was a journalist, she was unsurprised by my request. She did say she wasn't quite sure she would recognize me when she met me at the airport, but she reassured me that I would have no trouble identifying her—she would be wearing a sari.

The evening I arrived we talked till three in the morning. We knew little about each other. She had always been the shadowy aunt whom everybody felt faintly sorry for, and I'm sure that I was just one of the nieces she had heard about in casual conversation. But our rapport was immediate. We discovered a shared love of literature and of writing. In the course of my visit, I read almost all the clippings she had kept of her journalistic pieces, and delighted in her wit and sharp observations. She regaled me with stories of her contemporaries—poets, writers, musicians, journalists—who were now in India, and showed me articles she had written on them. But the work she was proudest of, she said, were her books for children, in Urdu. I met her friends, she asked me about mine in Lahore and Karachi. As so often happens on the subcontinent, we discovered many common acquaintances and, slowly, her life began to unfold for me. I asked her what she missed most about India, family apart. 'I miss the cultural life,' she replied. 'You know, they've crushed everything like that here. No dance, no music. Only qawwalis.'[2] She shuddered. I listened for hours to her recollections of Lucknow All India Radio where she had worked with artists like Akhtari Bai, Ali Akbar Khan, Ravi Shankar, and many others, now legendary. 'The cultural deprivation was something else,' she went on. 'I had brought my sitar, my tanpura, but my husband said you'd better hide them, people will say I've married a courtesan. I put them away, reluctantly. I was so fond of music, but I was aware that distinctions were being made.'

Through the nights that we talked I heard from her the Partition stories that were seldom told in our family, her own included. Stories of one who had stayed back, on the other side.

'You see,' she said, 'even now many Indians have not accepted Pakistan. There is a friend of mine in India whom I have been inviting to visit Pakistan, but she says she will visit Pakistan only when the two countries have become one, which of course means never. This is the meanest kind of possessiveness. We have to move on, we can't go back to the past.'

When she saw me off at Karachi airport, she hugged me tightly and asked, half-jokingly, 'So, how did you like your Pakistani aunt?'

Women's Oral History on Both Sides of Both Borders

In the mid-eighties in India, as also in Pakistan, Sri Lanka, Bangladesh, and Nepal, there was a ferment of activity in the women's movement around a host of issues. Among them were the creeping spectre of religious and ethnic intolerance and of violent conflict, as 'identity politics' threatened to engulf the subcontinent. Along with a large number of other groups working for progressive social change, we too tried to forge links with women's groups across our borders, and identify areas of shared concern. There were several. Setting aside the mutually hostile pronouncements—and actions—of our governments and politicians, we tried to make common cause on problems that transcended national political priorities. Such as our deteriorating environment. Increasing violence and militarization. Uneven development leading to greater poverty. Rising fundamentalism and intolerance. All these affected us very specifically as women, and although we were only too aware of our particular locations in our own contexts, we also recognized that there was a great need to try to neutralize animosity, especially between India and Pakistan, by demonstrating that it was possible to work together as common people, for the common good.

Over the years, there have been many exchanges and meetings between Indian and Pakistani groups on the environment, on child labour or trafficking, on women's rights, and with trade unions or displaced people. Theatre groups and media women, physicists against nuclearization, human-rights activists, civil liberties and democratic-rights groups have kept up a sporadic interaction. And one forum in particular, the Pak-India Forum for Peace and Democracy, has organized national conferences of several hundred people in both countries over the last five or six years.

At these levels, then, the dialogue has been quite open.

Already, in Karachi, I was beginning to wonder how I could possibly speak about women's experience of Partition without taking in their experiences on *both* sides of *both* borders—Punjab and Bengal. How one-sided and incomplete the picture would be without them, and how, otherwise, would I get around the vexatious question of borders and boundaries, except by posing it simultaneously from all three perspectives—Indian, Pakistani, and Bangladeshi—and by so doing, decentering nationalist historiography just a little. Just for a brief moment.

The decision to work on a collaborative oral history of women in Partition *from a combined perspective,* almost made itself. There would be five of us, two each in Pakistan and India, and one in Bangladesh. Nighat Said Khan and Anis Haroon lived and worked in Lahore and Karachi, respectively, and both their families had migrated to Pakistan—Nighat's from Rampur in north India, and Anis' from Hyderabad in central India. Kamla Bhasin and I, in

India, were from erstwhile West Punjab, she from Shahidanwali, and I from Lahore, and our families had moved to Rajasthan and Delhi in India in 1947. Salma Sobhan, our colleague in Dhaka, had the most interesting background of all. Her family had moved to Karachi from Calcutta in West Bengal and, subsequently, Salma moved with her husband to Dhaka, where she now lives. One way or another, we had all criss-crossed the country at some point in our lives. Moreover, we were all activists, shared broadly left politics, and were committed to the solidarity of the women's movement. As we discussed our project in Delhi, in Lahore and Karachi and in Dhaka, our excitement grew: after all, we had enough in common, not only in the past, but in present struggles too. So many different dimensions of Partition and its impact presented themselves that we began to feel that it was not only desirable to give it multiple, cross-border readings and meanings, but necessary. How else would we grasp the enormity of religious nationalism? Of linguistic or ethnic chauvinism? Of contesting and overlapping identities that have drawn and redrawn the map of south Asia in the intervening years?

A Multiplicity of Voices

Gender, community and nation in conflict. Not a new predicament, not likely to be just an old one either. In India, as we grappled with the scale and magnitude of Partition displacement and of how exactly the fact of division played itself out in people's lives, we began to encounter our own biases. Again and again we asked ourselves whether we were responding to stereo-typical accounts of Partition 'communally' and found, often, that even as we resisted stereotypes, we unwittingly reproduced them. Nationalist accounts of the nation, the only ones we had all been exposed to, are highly selective. As Cynthia Cockburn observed in the course of her work on Northern Ireland, Israel–Palestine, and Bosnia–Herzegovina:

... such renderings ... delete everything that does not contribute to the story of a unitary people. Their 'people' have a common origin, are like each other and different from others, march together along a given road, travelling towards a shared destiny. All the divergencies and convergences of real historic social time, the departures of some and arrivals of others, the mixing and splitting, the dyings-out and the illegitimate births are ignored.[3]

Although we tried to be self-consciously mindful of the 'divergencies and convergences', we nevertheless ended up making assumptions based on 'our' perceptions, rather than 'theirs'. For instance, for most Indians, Pakistan remains very much a part of south Asia, with a shared history and geography and many cultural resonances, especially in north India. For many Pakistanis, however, west Asia and the Middle East have become important cultural referents in the past few decades, and politically, they are clearly more significant than the subcontinent in many respects. As far as foreign policy and security issues are concerned, Pakistan in the eighties was more focused on Afghanistan and central Asia, while internally, its military rule and openly articulated Islamization encouraged a more 'Arabised' alignment.

We assumed that our research would continue to reflect not only our rootedness in a south Asian regional context, but also anticipate a future that could not be delinked from the past, that would have to contend with it in order to overcome it. With regard to our own subject, our shared assumption was that we would be able to subordinate our 'community' and 'national' identities to our gender identity, but this assumption was to unravel in unexpected ways. One characteristic of feminist oral history is that it places the question of one's own location at the heart of the enterprise. The very process of interviewing, the open-ended, non-directive approach that we adopted obviously altered our relationship with the women we spoke to, but it also churned up issues regarding our own identities, and forced us to confront them head-on.

Gradually, as the research and interviews got underway, our original plan had to be modified. We rearticulated the parameters of the project and revised the scope of our work in the light of our differing experiences and independent findings. Although our focus was still women, the Indian part of the enquiry concentrated on destitute women, on those who were abducted and recovered, and on their rehabilitation. The Pakistanis looked more closely at 'representative' samples of women in terms of class and community, fanned out into villages and examined the phenomenon of divided families. We still agreed on oral history as our preferred methodology, but agreed also that how we presented our interviews might differ. As our work progressed in India, we found that we were actually encountering a multiplicity of voices on the 'woman question'; this unexpected development ultimately led us to using a combination of archival material, government documents and reports, official and legal records, and legislative assembly debates in which to locate the women's accounts.

We began to think of, possibly, two companion volumes rather than a single one, presenting the findings of both studies as linked but separate. Indeed, this seemed to hold even greater promise as a strategy for collaborative work. But things were happening on the ground that militated against our joint effort. In the early nineties Karachi was in such turmoil with the Muhajir Qaumi Movement (MQM) that no one, women included, was willing to talk about 1947.[4] It became increasingly dangerous for the two Pakistani women working on the project to pursue their enquiry about the refugees of 1947 and resettlement programmes, or about violence against women, given the violence currently prevailing. Broaching the subject of Partition could trigger off suspicion or hostility, because the very status of the muhajirs (refugees) was predicated on an embattled identity. As Nighat Said Khan, one of our partners in Pakistan, noted, 'Sindi-Muhajir identities were being articulated through a violence that reminded migrants in Sind of the violence of Partition.' In India, much the same response greeted us in Amritsar: whenever we asked about 1948, for example, people immediately replied: '1984? In 1984, Operation Bluestar ...'[5] A symbolic inversion.

An early foray into West Bengal (India) and 'pilot' research in the resettled areas of Calcutta, in 1988, persuaded us that the Bengal experience too, needed to be studied on both sides of the border, because its post-Partition experience had been qualitatively different from the Punjab's. In some important respects, it is a continuing story as migrations from East Bengal/East Pakistan/Bangladesh are a current reality. But, even before we started our interviews, the Bengal part of the story had begun to recede. We were forced to accept—regretfully, as far as our project was concerned that for Bangladesh the defining moment was 1971: birth of a nation, freedom from Pakistan. If there was any history that needed to be recovered it was that of the movement for Sonar Bangla; 1947 almost didn't exist, except perhaps as the genesis of the struggles of 1971. Although it may well be the case that, as Ranabir Samaddar suggests, they have not been able to reconcile themselves to Partition, or as Dipesh Chakrabarty believes—that there is a 'stunned disbelief' that it could happen at all, Partition itself did not seem to be a research priority at the time. We could hardly insist that it become one.

The absence of women's voices from East Pakistan/Bangladesh in our study was a major loss, but since we had eschewed the practice of 'outsiders' interviewing 'subjects' on an experience as traumatic and intimate as this, all we could do was to hope that at some later date, someone else would be more successful. At the time, however, the full implications of its exclusion were not that evident to us. Shelley Feldman, writing about the invisibility of Bangladesh/East Pakistan in Partition historiography, argues that:

Understanding representations of the past requires engaging contemporary political interests, including constructions of communalism, difference, and critiques of the national narrative, using feminist and subaltern historiography as alternative modes of interpretation. My purpose is primarily a conceptual one, to acknowledge the exclusion and silence of the East Bengali voice in order to suggest how it has occurred and identify the epistemic foundations of the contemporary critique of the nationalist narrative. Until this exclusion of, and silence from, East Bengal is fully recognised for what it portends for the construction of the national narrative, whether of India, Pakistan or Bangladesh, it will be impossible to adequately recast the contemporary discourse on Partition. By exclusion I refer to the absence of the experiences of East Bengal in constructing the Indian and Pakistani narrative of Partition; by silence I mean the limited attention Bengalis and Bangladeshis pay to the Partition experience in building a nationalist consciousness and interpreting the struggle for Independence.

Although our attempt had, in fact, been to address the exclusion of, and silence from, East Bengal (albeit not as self-consciously as Feldman suggests), we were unable to do either.

The Imponderables of Cross-border Understanding

In 1998, ten years after the initial collaboration was first discussed (and, ironically. the same year that India and Pakistan imploded their nuclear devices), the Indian oral history was published in India and Pakistan, detailing the Indian part of the enquiry. To date, it remains the only one, although one essay on the Pakistan findings was published in 1994. In a very fundamental sense, our study is partial, 'incomplete', without the input that would have helped to construct a fuller, more accurate, and meaningful account of Partition from a gender perspective. So many questions remain unanswered: what did people really feel about the two-nation theory? How were they resettled? Did rehabilitation in Pakistan follow the same trajectory as in India? Or was it the case, as preliminary research indicted, that Waqf boards and community initiative were much more in evidence there? How was land redistributed? What happened to destitute women? Abducted women? How was the experience internalized? Recalled? Were the memories of ordinary people at variance with the official version, or of a piece with it? Were 'home' and 'homeland' synonymous? And, especially—how did those who still had family on the Indian side of the border negotiate the divide? What about those whose 'subliminal' identities accorded them a hyphenated status: Pakistani-not-Indian, not-Indian-not-Pakistani? People like my aunt who, when told she could be either Hindu or Muslim, replied, 'Either, neither or both.'

Too many imponderables. But the question that remains to haunt me is why we were unable to carry out our collaborative enquiry as we had hoped. It is a troubling one, both personally and politically, because in one sense it signified a failure of alliance. Difficult though it is—and, possibly, even undesirable—to try to understand why it happened, I feel it may be useful simply because so many of us still believe that the only way out of the impasse between our two countries is through similar endeavours. I say this, knowing how diplomats, power-brokers, politicians, and bureaucrats—the taxi driver's 'hukumat'—sitting across tables in the capitals of the region are often engaged in activities that are inimical to such processes, and may even perpetuate the impasse.

Was it ultimately personal differences or 'national differences' that confounded us? Did the latter overwhelm our similarities, or is it that what was articulated as personal differences flowed from our inability to bridge what Cynthia Cockburn calls the 'space between us?' By this, she means both the social space between women on either side of a conflictual or contested situation, as well as the physical and political space in which we live and work. It is true that, like the Women in Black who protested the aggression in former Yugoslavia, the four of us also had our own differences: of vantage point, of our understanding and experience of Partition, and of political positions on different issues. Even our feminism was not always a matter of accord.

In retrospect, I wonder whether on the Indian side, we were not inadvertently reproducing the 'Indian' response to the creation of Pakistan. As the research progressed, it became apparent that our preoccupation with it was of a different order, even though we had agreed that our common focus was on women. For us, Partition remained centre-stage, for the others, it seemed not to be. They had moved on, and so the nature of their enquiry was necessarily different. But this need not, by itself, have been an insurmountable difference; indeed, it was precisely this 'difference' that we hoped would afford us some insights into identity-formation, and perhaps even illuminate how misperceptions are created. Was it then that we had not been able to articulate 'difference' constructively? Nighat Said Khan has written that:

Our interest in this study was propelled by our involvement in the women's movement and by our preoccupation with the key concepts that this study was to explore—concepts which determine the nature and structure of Pakistani society. We were also drawn to it since we were unconvinced that Partition was necessarily the only resolution to the religious and communal problematic prior to 1947, and we were equally convinced that the 'false nationalisms' encouraged by the states of India and Pakistan were an affront to the feelings and aspirations of the people of both countries.

But, she continues,

We were acutely conscious that we were also the subjects of our study, and that in unravelling the many threads that clothed our view as Pakistanis, of Partition and of Pakistan, we were unravelling our selves.

Even as we worked, and as our 'separate' research compelled us to rephrase some of our concerns, the situation in our countries was changing rapidly. We were already in the early 1990s. Nighat Said Khan analysed it as follows:

During this period the world has changed. The New World Order has identified Islam as the 'other' in terms of global confrontation, and given voice to a Muslim identity in Muslims .... At the same time, the struggle in Kashmir has intensified, while India is going through a change that is bringing to the surface memories of pre-Partition India, with earlier perceptions of a 'Hindu' India and fears of 'Hindu rule'. This has meant that the responses that we got in 1987 changed during this period, and while many of the earlier responses, especially on the specificity of Partition and the violence that surrounded it, are still valid, the dominant identity emerging in migrants from India, especially in urban Sind and urban Punjab at the moment, is of being a Muslim.

The exigencies of contemporary identity-formation affected the course of her research much more decisively than it did ours, although we could not escape it either.

At the time, I must admit, her reading of what was emerging in India did not quite cohere with ours, and it seemed to us that 'national' or 'local' manifestations of identity politics, whether in Sind or Punjab or Kashmir, would have to be negotiated by us, independently of our 'common' project. It is obvious to me now that these 'separations' are much more difficult to deal with than we anticipated, because these processes impinge on each of us, individually and jointly. (To undertake a similar collaboration today, on Partition, has quite different implications for us in India, because the Hindu right is resurrecting the experience in an extremely divisive and negative manner.)

Cynthia Cockburn has identified six important factors in any cross-border alliance on conflict work, one of which, she claims, is 'non-closure' of identity. So, she says, identities cannot be 'essentialized', there must be a great willingness on everyone's part to 'wait and see', to believe that there may be many ways of living one's identity. But these identities are also 'relational' and, importantly, 'changeable', and one follows upon the other. Because 'a social formation has so many structured differentiations, potential categories of inclusion and exclusion, belonging and alienation, the self is seen as potentially very complex, shaped through many attachments.'

Our location in the women's movement and commitment to our research agenda notwithstanding, our complex 'selves' could not find the time or the necessary space—personal and political—for a satisfactory, painstaking understanding of our predicament to emerge. In other words, we found that it was not enough to forge a politics of solidarity: what we need is a 'politics of understanding' between people, accompanied by a 'politics of accommodation among nations'. Nighat expressed it poignantly, 'The trauma of Partition lingers within me, a Partition made more real by my experiences while doing this work. I begin to understand it.'

The Elusive Transnational Perspective

On 8 March 2000, a busload of Indian women activists from different walks of life travelled to Lahore in a gesture of solidarity with Pakistani women, and as a public expression of people-to-people diplomacy and bridge-building. The following month, two busloads of Pakistani women teachers, journalists, lawyers, theatre people, politicians, and students arrived in Delhi in affirmation of that gesture and statement. Asma Jehangir, organizer of the group said, in response to a question by the press, that if the border at Wagah (Punjab) were thrown open, there would be queues of people on either side stretching for miles, waiting in line to cross over.

Just as the taxi driver said.

This is the conundrum of India–Pakistan relations: the almost simultaneous hostility and cordiality that are neither mutually exclusive nor impossibly contradictory. Often they seem to run parallel to each other, exemplifying if you like, the 'gap' between 'hukumat' and 'awam', between 'governments' and 'people'. Yet one must be wary of oversimplification. The antagonism is real enough, and growing. Hawks will—and do—say that we have much to be antagonistic about. Muslim and Hindu religious nationalists have both, according to Mushirul Hasan, 'appropriated the British divide-and-rule paradigm' of oppositional, separate, civilisational entities which cannot survive peacefully in the same space. Though such convictions run completely counter to centuries of experience of harmonious co-existence, through all the 'intricate and fascinating processes of interaction' between living religions and cultures in the subcontinent, they have nevertheless managed to polarize attitudes and entrench misperceptions.

In such a context, was it then foolhardy of us to think that we could work collaboratively on an action-research project, on a subject as charged as Partition? Perhaps it was, but the rejoinder to that must be: how long can we continue to fruitfully examine it from our perspective alone? Despite our earlier disappointment, it seems to me to be even more important now to approach the vexed and contentious question of identities from distinct but sympathetic positions, in a spirit of co-operation that is alert to all the yawning gaps that 'national differences' and coercive identity politics confront us with.

The legacy of Partition for all three countries is, ultimately: the fragility of nations; the porosity of borders; the reality of migration. The *migrant/refugee/ muhajir*—the person displaced—has become the new metaphor of the subcontinent. In Tayyab Mahmud's words,

As a cultural signifier (the migrant) is to be erased. As a violator of borders, she provides the rationale to ever strengthen the territorial divides .... She calls into question cultural homogeneity, linguistic commonality, shared history, a sense of belonging and security of identity—the key ideologies of the nation.

In other words, she could as easily be you—or me. If we accept this possibility then, as June Jordan says, 'The final risk or final safety lies within each of us attuned to the messy and intricate and unending challenge of self-determination.'

Notes

1. Research Analysis Wing and Inter-Services Intelligence, external intelligence agencies of the Indian and Pakistani governments, respectively.

2. Sufi chants (editor's note).

3. Cynthia Cockburn, *The Space Between Us: Negotiating Gender and National Identities in Conflict* (London: Zed Books, 1998), p. 228.

4. The MQM, a movement of Urdu-speaking refugees from 1947 was agitating for rights and entitlements in Sind, which they believed had been denied to them by successive governments in Punjab.

5. Operation Bluestar was a military take-over in June 1984 of the Golden Temple in Amritsar (Punjab), believed to be the hideout of the extremist, Sant Bhindrawale, agitating for a separate Sikh state. The temple itself was being used as an arsenal, and the shootout led to the death of Bhindrawale. Eventually, it was also responsible for the assassination of Mrs Indira Gandhi on 31 October 1984.

Women's Trauma and Triumph

SUBHORANJAN DASGUPTA

It was neither an historian nor a theorist of history who first proposed a new reading of the Partition of the subcontinent. The need for an alternative or even counter-narrative was first felt by the novelist Jyotirmoyee Devi, who in her classic novel on the Partition, *Epar Ganga Opar Ganga*, published in 1967, demanded that attention be focused on the millions who suffered on account of the Partition, rather than on the few who engineered it. Obviously, Jyotirmoyee Devi wanted to concentrate on the trauma women had to face, and she dedicated her novel to the persecuted and abused women of all countries and all ages. She must also have been keenly aware of the historical validity of her work, or else she would not have permitted its publication in *Probasi*, in 1966, under the meaningful title *Itihase-Stree Parba*—or 'Woman's Phase in History'. In the preface, she condemned the myopic bias of all Grand Narratives: 'Even the great Vedavyasa did not write the real *Stree-Parba*, he merely touched on the terrible tale at places ... That *Stree-Parba* has yet to be written.' Sutara Datta, her protagonist in the novel, accused the deity of history of remaining deaf and mute. This deity, Sutara insisted, remained indifferent to the fate of thousands of women who were tyrannized and tormented in both Punjab and Bengal. Sutara herself embodied the trauma and triumph of Partition, as experienced by countless women. She lost almost everything because of Partition, but then fought back stubbornly to regain love and compassion—in short, faith in life.

Jyotirmoyee Devi's rightful demand for a new human history of Partition is nothing more nor less than what James Young calls the 'activity of telling history itself'. Moreover, when we urge women—victims, sufferers, and fighters—to narrate this history either in creative terms or as oral witnesses, we follow the famous precept of Joan Kelly who wanted to 'restore women to history and history to women'. That is precisely what Urvashi Butalia has accomplished in her remarkable book *The Other Side of Silence* and what Ritu Menon and Kamla Bhasin have done in their joint effort entitled *Borders and Boundaries—Women in India's Partition*. They have, so to speak, ransacked history, excavated memory, prompted the sufferers to speak and, in the process, written that counter-narrative which is contra-history itself.

Counter-narrative

This history, nourished by the collective memory of the thousands of up-rooted women of Punjab, is not only existential to the core, but essential in its ethical import. The testimony of the women whom we have spoken to and will speak to in the near future is creating anew history of Partition which, with its human content, is challenging what Jyotirmoyee Devi—and Gyanendra Pandey after her—describe as the 'politics of history'. The mas-ter-narrative of Partition, if there is one, has failed to speak to us in the voice of women uprooted, raped, molested, humiliated and even doubted, and rejected by their own people; of their setting up new homes, finding new workplaces, and gaining new political consciousness.

Evidently, these lacunae may be filled by the voices of the survivors themselves who saw through it all. They provide a new kind of evidence, based on infallible experience, and to that extent they enjoy, ironically, a privileged epistemic position. In his excellent article 'The Survivor in the Study of Violence', Amrit Srinivasan has valued this position as 'mediating life and death, chaos and order, speech and silence'. Further, the researcher, with the help of the survivor, 'smuggles the social structure into his studies, through the backdoor as it were'. An increasing dependence on this history on the margin or history through the backdoor has recently provoked misgivings in some quarters. Those who are to a large extent influenced by the Heideggerian categories of Being and Forgetting have questioned the reliability of Memory and also the veracity of the witness. In simple terms, they warn that oral evidence could well nigh turn out to be patently false or at least mired in half-truths. But, even after accepting this risk of being waylaid, we also need to stress in emphatic terms that so far, those who have spoken have not deceived us. We make this claim for the following reasons: (i) not many were willing to speak; (ii) some flatly refused; (iii) those who ultimately spoke had to be persuaded; (iv) not all questions fetched answers; (v) we were pointedly asked to conceal the identity of some speakers; (vi) not a single witness tried to sound brave, heroic, or grandiloquent; (vii) almost everyone adopted the undertone or the tone of restraint; and (viii) the real witnesses who are now old and at times decrepit have nothing whatsoever to gain by uttering half-truths. Their restraint was so palpable that even when describing the attacks during the communal riots, the name of the assaulting community was often replaced by a simple 'Ora' or 'they'.

Women's Testimony in Brindabon

Even this 'Other' was dropped by the eighty-six-yearold Ela Bandyopadhyay. Her broken sentences uttered in 'Amar Bari', a home for aged women in Brindabon, depended only on unadorned verbs to recall the tragedy and trauma of the past. This is what she had to say: 'My in-laws had their home in Brandipara village in Jessore. My husband was a doctor, he was well-placed. I had three sons—the eldest was in Matric class, the next in class five, and the youngest in class four. It was 1947, they went to the market and did not return. No trace of them. Then the house was attacked and also the dispensary. When my husband came to know everything, he decided, 'We shall leave today'. We left at night, entered Bongaon. Then he said, 'No more samsar,[1] let us go to Brindabon, we shall die there'. He found shelter in Pagalbaba's *Ashram* and I used to chant Hari's name in a dharamsala. Since 1947, we have only pronounced Hari's name. No relative has come, we know nothing else. We salvaged some peace in Brindabon. My husband died ten years ago. I pray, I have my Gopal, I don't want to go anywhere.' There is not a trace of embellishment in this skeletal reconstruction of memory. Ela Bandyopadhyay is not alone in Brindabon. 297 women came to Brindabon from East Bengal between 1947 and 1948; they embody the collective trauma of Partition. They were followed by others who came during the 1950s and even after the emergence of Bangladesh.

In 'Amar Bari', we spoke to Radhadasi Baidya, seventy years old, who came to Brindabon in 1972; to Kiranbala Halder, seventy years old, who left her village Hausdi in Faridpur district in the mid-fifties; to Gopika Saha, sixty-six years old, who left Noakhali in 1960; to Chapalasundari Dhar, ninety years old, who left Dakhinbari village in Noakhali in 1947; to Sushila De, eighty years old, who left Habiganj in 1946. They all actualized history without exaggerating it, and as we spoke to them, one by one, the past as it had been in Noakhali, Faridpur, Jessore, and Dhaka was resurrected. The past on this side was equally grim as narrated by Kiranbala Halder: 'The riots were terrible. We ran away—my husband, two daughters, and I. Somehow, we managed to set up a hut in Kalna. But, as fate would have it, my husband disappeared. I was forced to come to Calcutta, live in a *bustee* and work as a maid. I worked hard, the daughters grew up and I got them married. But then living with my married daughters was a terrible experience. I have suffered a lot, no more. That's why I have come here. I'll chant Radha-Krishna in Brindabon till I die.'

Ela Bandyopadhyay and Kiranbala Halder have succumbed to Radha-Krishna as their last refuge. There is no glint of triumph in this devotion or surrender. Nevertheless, we detected a strange quality of moral victory in Chapalasundari Dhar's narration. This ninety-year-old woman was married at the age of eleven, lost her husband when she was only fourteen and thereafter lived with her brothers. A resident of Brindabon for the last forty years she said, 'I came here willingly. You see, I am a child-widow. I don't even know what conjugal life means, so I don't have any craving. I care for my Radharani, I am happy. I have only one desire in my life: I would like to see Anusuya—the young supervisor of this home—happily married. But, her husband should stay here, so that Anusuya does not have to leave.' Chapalasundari experienced '*Noakhali*', widowhood, isolation—yet, while she spoke, she laughed merrily. Her source of strength and joy appeared to be impregnable. Whenever we examine this evidence, we are reminded of James Young's verdict, which he pronounced after speaking to victims and witnesses of the Shoah: 'Unlike written history that tends to hide its lines of construction, oral testimonies retain the process of construction, the activity of witness.'

Calcutta Between Trauma and Triumph

If Brindabon represents the tormented margin of the impact of Partition on women who had been displaced, and later sought solace in religion, then Calcutta and its suburbs represent the heartland where the epic battle was fought between trauma and triumph. No one emerged a clear victor in this battle. While many like Nita in Ritwik Ghatak's *Meghe Dhaka Tara* desperately struggled to live; or, like Pari in Salil Sen's play *Natun Yehudi* were compelled to accept the primrose path, thousands of others waged a simultaneous battle on three fronts: they toiled along with men to build up new homes from almost nothing; they fought alongside their male relatives to drive off the goondas of landlords; and, last but not least, they acquired the necessary skill and expertise to earn money outside their homes. This hefty struggle waged by the uprooted women of East Bengal has gone mostly unsung, though it has received a deathless symbol in Nita in *Meghe Dhaka Tara*. More importantly, the daredevil attitude of these women, challenging goondas with sticks and brooms, and venturing out in buses and trams to work, encouraged the reserved and withdrawn women of West Bengal to follow suit. In due course, the psyche and physiognomy of the urban Bengali woman changed—Partition prompted her to embrace the role of the bread-earner.

When American researcher Rachel Weber came to Calcutta to study the role of women in the development of refugee colonies in Calcutta, she was also struck by the paucity of writing on this vibrant subject, although, to use her words, 'their presence pervades Calcutta's economic, cultural and political life'. She, too, had to depend on Prafulla Chakrabarti's *Marginal Men*, Nilanjana Chatterjee's articles on the exodus and, of course, on the absorbing celluloid accounts of Ritwik Ghatak. But no existing record was comprehensive enough to capture the dimension of the coerced migration. It was claimed officially, that thirty-five lakh refugees came from East Bengal between 1946 and 1950 and that thousands of them crossed over, primarily, to save their womenfolk. Fear of rape and dishonour of women was, in fact, one of the major reasons for this massive displacement. Yet, surprisingly enough, this very upheaval which apparently protected the honour of some women threw the old order of life into chaos. It provoked new rhythms which revised the terms and demands of women's engagement in quest of new forms of legitimation, including reconstruction of the home, 'basa' in compensation for the lost homeland; a do-or-die political movement inspired by Leftists which not only concentrated on sudden land-grabbing movements but also encouraged the uprooted to participate in rallies, demonstrations, and violent agitations; joining the wage-labour force with grit and determination. This 'coming out' was hailed as a liberating experience. An activist who experienced these sea-changes told Rachel Weber: 'Tradition, culture and customs were all left behind. In the new environment, women worked outside and spoke to unknown men ... Values changed. Women were once illiterate and backward. They spent all of their time cooking and gossiping. In Calcutta they went out on the streets.' It would be wrong to state that only women of East Bengal displayed this steely resolve. Refugees who had poured in from West Pakistan also battled to establish themselves. Urvashi Butalia summed up this entire process by saying, 'Just as a whole generation of women were destroyed by Partition, so also Partition provided an opportunity for many to move into the public sphere in a hitherto unprecedented way'. Rachel Weber, in her otherwise excellent article, wrongly characterizes this movement into the public sphere as an expansion of refugee women's domestic realm. Yet it was something much more than that. In point of fact, it was the dramatic opening of a new realm which paved the way for future generations of Bengali working women and activists.

In our conversations with displaced women, activists, and social workers we focused on this crucial aspect of socio-economic transformation. Manju Chattopadhyay, a college lecturer, who taught female students who had crossed over from East Bengal, had this to say: 'Girls from East Bengal came out on the streets because they had to. They protected their homes, went to schools and colleges and made a beeline for jobs after acquiring the minimum qualification. When the trade unions agreed to recruit women for white collar jobs, girls of East Bengal responded with fervour—they became typists, stenographers, salesclerks. They had to face a lot of criticism then because their past and present had made them rough and impolite. But they simply did not care. This image of the refugee-girl working and earning prompted the once-demure girls of West Bengal to do the same. It is time to admit that uprooted girls from East Bengal inspired those who were rooted here to seek new, living forms of identity and assertion.'

Women's New-found Political Activism

Manju Chattopadhyay led us to Sukumari Chaudhuri, who serves as a glowing paradigm of the 'Partition woman'. Sukumari lost her first husband in the Noakhali riots of 1946; she criss-crossed between East and West for sometime and ultimately settled in the West in 1950 when riots flared up again in Barisal. She lived for five years in a 'jabardhakal'—or forcibly occupied—colony, then joined Nari Seba Sangha to train herself for a job and was employed at Bengal Lamp where she waged a militant struggle as a worker. While working there, she married a trade-union leader who initiated her into leftist politics. Sukumari Chaudhury, who now lives alone in her little house in Santoshpur, recalled her past in a matter-of-fact tone:

After receiving training at Nari Seba Sangha, I joined Bengal Lamp in 1953–4. At first, there were no more than ten or twelve women workers. But then several women's organisations trained women from East Bengal who joined. Soon, there were about 150 women working. Our job at first was to make filament for bulbs. Well, our salaries were meagre. So, we had to agitate for a bonus before the *Pujas*. Women agitated with fervour and were guided by the then-undivided Communist Party. I do not know whether I should call myself a militant, that is for others to judge. But we did fight for six long months. During the long period of strikes, the employers tried to use agents and *goondas* against us. When the police came to arrest me, I told the officer, 'I shall catch you by your belt and throw you into the pond'. It is true that I lost everything in East Bengal, but still I do not nurture any ill-feeling for any particular community. My life, especially my political experience and training did not permit me to become communal.

A portrait of Lenin adorns a wall of Sukumari Chaudhuri's house; she goes regularly to the local temple to listen to 'Ramkatha' and her house is open to young Bangladeshis. Even when she excavates the past she remains un-ruffled—the mayhem at Noakhali and the agitation at Bengal Lamp never cause her to raise her voice. Yet, at the existential level, she speaks on behalf of thousands of women who, like her, lost their dear ones during the Partition years, crossed over to save their honour, fought adamantly to retain their homes in *jabardhakal* colonies, participated energetically in political agitations, acquired skills to become wage-earners, challenged the might of factory-owners and police, exhibited the courage to marry for the second time and build a home again. Sukumari Chaudhury, like Ritwik Ghatak's heroine Nita, wanted to defy the odds—and she succeeded.

That this resurgence of the Partition woman was steered to a large extent by Communist politicians and workers is no longer disputed. Leading women in the then-undivided Communist Party found enthusiastic comrades in the colonies as a common vision of emancipation brought the two groups close to each other. Describing this communion, Manikuntala Sen, a famous Communist activist, wrote in her memories *Sediner Katha*:

We began acquiring new friends, one after another, from the colonies. I rediscovered my old acquaintances from East Bengal and, moreover, established ties with new 'sisters' and 'aunts' who joined the Mahila Samiti. New organisations and *samitis* sprung up in these colonies. Renu Ganguly, Kamala, Kabita, Basanti emerged as organisers and soon turned out to be excellent workers. They all joined the Party later. They struggled hard and turned each and every colony into an impregnable fortress. I did not want to return from these colonies. It is as if I found my lost Barisal there.

Not only those who lived in refugee colonies in and around Calcutta, but also female members of lower-middle-class families who struggled against despair and poverty in tiny, suffocating one-room shelters, decided to work in order to earn money. The trauma of their grinding poverty prompted them to venture out, determined to change the conditions which stifled them. One such indefatigable fighter is the talented actress Sabitri Chatterjee, who had to leave her prosperous home in Dhaka along with other members of her family. Sabitri Chatterjee insists in her memoirs that she was neither a penniless refugee, in the accepted sense of term, nor did she ever live in a refugee colony. Nevertheless, her family had to bear gnawing poverty and Sabitri Chatterjee had to earn money, like any other refugee girl, when she was only twelve years old. Ironically, her life as an actress began when she was chosen to play the role of a refugee girl in Salil Sen's play *Natun Yehudi*. These 'Natun Yehudis' (or new Jews) were none other than East Bengalis uprooted from their native soil. Sabitri Chatterjee was not given a penny for her acting, though *Natun Yehudi* turned out to be a great success. She also joined a touring dance company to help her family. While describing this struggle, the actress did not sentimentalize; in fact, she recalled wryly:

In order to earn five or ten rupees. I took part in the crowd scenes. That was also an experience. I had to stand in a long queue with others outside the studio and if I was preferred, the chance came. I only used to get five rupees, the remaining five rupees went to the agent, for that was the rule. But even those five rupees were so important for my family. During that period of bitter struggle we almost forgot that we once had a big house in Kamalapur in Dhaka, that my father was well-placed and generous in East Bengal. We could not even imagine poverty in Dhaka until it struck us full in Calcutta in that nightmare of our shelter. Let me confess. I left no stone unturned to procure a role. I went to so many people—producers, directors, actors—and to everyone I said, 'please, give me a chance'. I cannot count the number of doors I knocked on. I still remember one supplier of extras, after hearing my appeal, began to laugh. He advised me to look in the mirror.

But this miserable experience failed to destroy Sabitri who described herself as 'limitlessly adamant'. Ultimately she won and her success as an actress proved that the 'Natun Yehudi' could also triumph.

Sabitri Chatterjee is one of the few actresses of Bengal who has fared remarkably well on the stage as well as on the screen. She teamed up with Uttam Kumar in the popular play *Shyamali,* where she played the role of a speechless woman for two and a half hours. The poet Jasimuddin went into raptures after seeing her performance for which she would make 500 rupees per show, while the great Uttam Kumar got 350. Like many other bread-earners of her time, Sabitri Chatterjee, immersed in the job of sustaining her family, ignored her own desires and inclinations. She did not marry. Her recollection ends on a note of wistful regret:

From unpaid dancer to lowly-paid actress performing for amateur clubs—what have I not done to maintain my family. I rose from that level. Money and fame ultimately came, my days turned bright ... yet I lament at times. I was caught up so intensely in that race to exist that I did not pause to think about myself, about my own family which I might have raised. Not all blessings are showered on everyone. Even without being aware of it, attainable bliss slips from the palms of some people.

Sabitri Chatterjee is not alone in this regard. We have come across quite a few sisters or '*didis*', who, after crossing over to the western side, devoted themselves completely to the task of bringing up the younger ones. They performed the preordained function of males in an otherwise male-dominated society, and in the process snuffed out their own feminine longings. They stamped out gender-discrimination in order to survive.

A Dialectical Bond

What is the basic structure of emotion which distinguishes these Partition women? What is the unifying bond between Somavanti in the West and Sukumari Chaudhury in the East, Chapalasundari in Brindabon and Sabitri Chatterjee in Calcutta? It is essentially dialectical, operating between the two extreme points of trauma and triumph. Neither ultimately prevails over the other. For whenever trauma terminates, its memory mellows the quality of triumph or reconciliation. As Somavanti told Kamla Bhasin and Ritu Menon: 'Even today there is no peace. No peace outside, nor peace inside. There is no peace even today. I don't sleep, there is a feeling of being unsettled.' But, at the same time, this intrinsic disquiet provoked by memory did not thwart the inherent will to live. Both coalesced to create an emotion true to the kindred points of loss and recovery, fall and redemption. Memories, oral evidence, as well as creative statements on Partition, explore this tense conflict and resolve that the experience of Partition, defying the violence and death it summoned, appealed to life as its only refuge. Nita, the unforgettable heroine of *Megha Dhaka Tara* filled the hills and fields with her echoing call 'I want to live'. This same refrain of life is heard in *Tamas* when the characters cry 'O Rabba'. Explaining the significance of this word, Govind Nihalani, the director of *Tamas* said: 'It is a cry for help, cry for strength, cry of a human being who wants to live'. Indeed, the broken fragments of any discourse on Partition are held together by this litany for life. When we speak to the dramatis personae of this cataclysm, we are inevitably reminded of the two memorable lines of Paul Celan, who, in his description of another cataclysm wrote, 'I hear that the axe has flowered ... I hear that they call life our only refuge.'

Notes

1. Chain of reincarnations. (editor's note).

Asymmetrical Nationhood in India and Pakistan*

MUSHIRUL HASAN

In this interview, Indian historian Mushirul Hasan discusses both the success and failure of secular nationalism in India—a failure consummated by the partition of India and Pakistan in 1947. Yet Hasan is far more critical of the illusory notion of a homogeneous Muslim community, which, he affirms, lies at the root of the partition of Pakistan and Bangladesh in 1971. As he points out, communitarian identity is itself a recent historical construct, whose roots lie in the British colonial administration's inability to accommodate diversity. Yet communities cannot be wished away. Rather than aiming at an unattainable level of integration, he argues in favour of a social contract sensitive to diversity.

As an historian, you have written both on the subject of partition and on the Muslim community in India. More recently, you have taken an interest in family histories. How do you see your own methodological development within your discipline?

Mushirul Hasan: The major shift took place immediately after my under-graduate degree at the Aligarh Muslim University in India, where I had studied medieval Indian history—that is, the period from the thirteenth to roughly the eighteenth century. I subsequently shifted my research, most of which I started at the University of Cambridge, to what, in India, we call 'communal politics'. At the time, in 1974, I was not particularly interested in

---

* An interview by Rada Iveković and Ghislaine Glasson Deschaumes.

the Partition of India: it was not something that was being debated in academic circles. Besides, the division of the country had not affected my family or me. I was born after Pakistan was created, no members of my family had migrated there, so there were no memories.

My interest in the nationalist movement developed under my father's influence, a historian of considerable repute. As a liberal father and a progressive historian. he encouraged us to debate both historical and contemporary issues. He sensitized me to the broadly secular and supracommunal movement. And yet he talked about the differences that set Hindus and Muslims apart and eventually culminated in the bitter, brutal, and violent partition of the country. As I moved to Delhi to commence my research—I was only twenty years old—I asked myself a simple and straightforward question: why did secular nationalism fail in India? This question assumed some degree of significance particularly because my teachers at Aligarh had written extensively on the multicultural character of Indian society, the fusion of Hindu and Muslim cultural traditions, and the pluralist heritage of our society. Why, then, did everything fall apart?

Turning to the archival materials, one was quick to discern several trends and tendencies that led various Muslim groups to express their anxieties, question the claim of the Indian National Congress, founded in 1885, to represent the nation, and eventually demand a separate Muslim homeland.

My chief contribution, if I may say so, has been to examine the complex role that a whole galaxy of Muslim political leaders, intellectuals, and other luminaries have played in the making of modern India. Second, I have questioned, for the first time in a rigorous manner, the very notion of a homogenized, monolithic Muslim community. This line of questioning has important historical and sociological implications. Long before I wrote my first book, sociologists had talked about the social stratification amongst Muslims at a theoretical level, but I worked it out in different regions, in different epochs. Finally, I write firmly from within a nationalist strand of Indian historiography but without the complacencies and conceits of that strand. Rather, I interrogate a number of intersections: between nationalism and communalism, between the communal and secular trends within the national movement, between Muslim nationalists and advocates of the Pakistan movement, and now, increasingly, between political history and literary history as alternative and overlapping modes of access to the social consciousness of an age.

Historically and politically speaking, who actually profited from this process of homogenization of the Muslim community that you critiqued?

MH: All said and done, the homogenization of the Muslims as a community or a distinct political category was initially the work of the British government. In a sense, the British created a sense of communitarian identity: by asking you what your religion was, what your past was, what your tribe was, and so on. These were new constructions. The idea of being a Muslim, or being a Brahman, existed in pre-British times—there is no question about that. But, the homogenization of these categories was a British invention. More important still is that the construction of this Muslimness was translated into formal constitutional arrangements. In other words, Muslims were given preferential treatment in the power structures to legitimize their separate and distinct identity.

It may be overstating the case to argue that the British invented it; perhaps colonialism merely provided the framework for it to take place. After all, it was not so much an administrative decision as the whole social, economic, and political context which allowed these latent identities to gel. Do you think this sort of institutionalization of difference could be described as a specific feature of British colonialism?

MH: There is obviously a very stark difference between British colonialism in India and in Malay or Kenya. There is no other country as culturally, socially, ethnically, and linguistically diverse as India. The British were obviously struck by this diversity; they were also dealing with a country with a rich civilization. Both the richness and the diversity created enormous problems, from a purely administrative and governmental perspective. And the only way the British could make sense of the society was to split it into these arbitrary categories; that is what the census did—to evolve a more disaggregated form of Indian society. The census didn't just remain on paper, by the way. It was translated into practice, into formal institutional arrangements. This is a perfect example of political identity being thrust upon a community which was otherwise diverse, fractured, and stratified.

In a way, then, the British were fulfilling a need for representation; it was the only way they could deal with reality.

MH: It was a result of British efforts to accommodate what they regarded as the dominant interest groups in Indian society. They proceeded in the same way with the princes, the land-owning families, and, though very begrudgingly, with the Muslims. Let's not forget that the British representation of the Muslims up until the 1860s or 1870s was a very hostile one—comparable to the representation of Islam today in Europe. But political expediency demanded this negative image of Islam be set aside and an attempt be made to draw the Muslims—who made up nearly one-third of the population of British India—into the colonial framework.

There has been a very thorough-going shift in French historiography, stemming from the 'new history' movement, which has entailed a shift of interest toward family histories, local history, and so on. Though it remains in the field of historiography, this micro-history contributes a whole new quality to the findings, not least of all because the position of the historian shifts, and plays a more modest role. How do you see your methodological shift to family histories?

MH: It is all part of the same journey, though, at the micro-level. I see family history linked with larger questions of social history and identity. What I want to do is to draw out certain larger, magisterial conclusions, which would make sense not only in understanding the history of the family but in delineating the social contours of that region.

Subaltern studies have provided a major advance on existing interpretations. I am not part of that movement, but do not see myself as hostile to the Subalterns. However, they have not been able to come to terms with the kinds of questions that concern me as a political and social historian. The theme of communitarian identity, the theme of ethnicity, the story of Partition has so far eluded most Subaltern historians. Not all the Subalterns are historians, by the way, though, fortunately, the formal distinction between political scientists, sociologists, and historians has now more or less disappeared.

When the fatwa came down on Salman Rushdie's novel, you took a position against banning books ...

MH: Yes, my troubles began in April 1992 when I took an unequivocal stand against the banning of books. That triggered violence and agitation; the university was shut, examinations postponed. And then the government set up a committee to look into the incident. The committee's report was subsequently placed before Parliament, and on the basis of that report, I returned to the university in December 1992. That is when I was assaulted. I was unable to return to the university for the next four years. I only returned to the university as its officiating vice-chancellor in October 1996, under heavy police protection. After so much agony and suffering, life has finally returned to normal. I teach at the same university, write my books and my fortnightly column in a leading national newspaper. The agitation against me stiffened my resolve to raise my voice against intolerance and religious victory.

Do you think your assailants were students of the university or outside elements?
MH: They were students, teachers, and professional politicians. Sadly, some of my own colleagues were happy to see me battered and bruised. Yet, I was triumphant; they were made to look silly in the eyes of the world.

Were they sent away?
MH: I was sent away, not them! In our society, the victim is often at the receiving end. I am treated as a 'controversial' figure and not the assailants or the organisers of the ill-advised agitation. The guilty are rewarded, while a person who took a stand consistent with our constitution was dismissed as 'controversial'. This is how the liberal voice in our society gets stifled.

Did you subsequently take a position in favour of other writers faced with the same type of fatwa?
MH: I wasn't asked to: once bitten twice shy!

Let's turn to Partition: independence came about through violence, and two countries were created, though not on the same principle. India is a secular country, whereas Pakistan was created on the basis of a presumed religious identity. Pakistan was premised on the two-nation theory, which was not an Indian idea. It is something of an historical irony that although the two-nation theory was false at the outset (because it did not correspond to the reality of India at the time), after fifty years it has turned out to be a self-fulfilling prophecy. Thus, we are now faced with two asymmetrical nations, different from the Pakistani idea of two nations, in that the Indian Muslims chose to belong to the Indian nation and not to the Muslim nation. India has a Muslim community—120 million people—which is part and parcel of the Indian nation.
MH: Basically, the movement for Pakistan rested on ill-founded assumptions. Yet the Pakistan movement was, in the 1940s and not earlier, a massive, popular movement for separation. We must recognize that the two-nation idea was transformed into a reality, a painful one. Immediately after Partition, Mohammad Ali Jinnah made a plea for a secular state. But his plea was a case of too little, too late. Having triggered the kind of passions that he did, there was no question of Pakistan emerging as a secular society. The important thing is that Pakistan's search for identity has really been constrained by the presence of so many diverse and antagonistic groups and their

conflicting interests. It is not the emergence of Bangladesh in 1971 which necessarily disproves the two-nation theory, but rather the way in which Pakistan's journey, beginning 14 August 1947, has been hampered by so many conflicts and contradictions. Though you can fault the Indian nationalist movement on several counts, the vision nursed by the nationalist leaders from the last quarter of the nineteenth century onward was a unified vision in which different castes and communities had a place.

Could you go into more detail about how both these nationalisms failed, and about the failure of homogeneous Muslim nationalism?
MH: Nationalism at any given point of time exhausts itself. It has happened in the case of a lot of societies. It has happened in the case of Yugoslavia and the Soviet federal state. The difference is that Indian nationalism did not exhaust itself as fast as other nationalisms did; it actually served as a major catalyst for bridging the gap between different groups, castes, regions, and communities. When I talk of the failure of Indian nationalism, I mean the poor representation of the under-classes and their social and economic backwardness; the treatment meted out to women; the growing fears of minority groups; and the slow progress of our economy. Those are clear illustrations of failure.

Today, Hindu fundamentalism, which often dons the mask of universalism, points to problems within Indian secular nationalism. But don't we require a more strenuous definition of nationhood? In my understanding, a nation is a community; and a community is a vertical construction, not a democratic one. Whereas a society is secular, a nation—that is, a religious-communitarian construct—is not. Over the long term, the question arises as to how to make a society out of a nation.
MH: Secular experimentation in the West was the result of certain tangible social and economic forces. If you look at Britain after the Industrial Revolution, or France after the French Revolution, or Germany after unification, though individuals may have acted as a catalyst, the whole secular fabric in Europe emerged from these major movements which were not geographically or territorially confined. The process was very different in India, where the creation of a nation was embedded in the nationalist project itself. India was not yet a nation at the end of the nineteenth century. What was unique in India was the way in which creating a nation became the blueprint of a major nationalist project. (Obviously the idea of nationalism and nationhood was also the consequence of a perception of exploitation by British colonialism, but that is not an aspect that I am touching on here.)

Furthermore, to carry out the project, there had to be a recognition of pluralism. The recognition of a multi-cultural society has been the bedrock—and hence the strength—of the nationalist movement. The secret behind Gandhi's enormous popularity, for example, was his ability to communicate the idea of nationhood. He was obviously sensitive to the enormous difficulties in translating this idea into practice, but the moral and political philosophy he developed lay at the heart of his attempt to unify the different segments of the population. In other words, nationalism became a crucial part of the daily experiences of the Indian people, partly because of their suffering under colonialism, and partly because the nationalist leaders placed before them a goal which seemed at once distant, yet realizable, and which in the end proved quite effective. The problem with this grand project was the failure to accord the communities their just place in the sorts of arrangements that were being worked out—because that was not a notion that the protagonists of Indian nationalism were able to come to terms with. The idea was that communities would be integrated into this coherent whole that was assiduously being built—but communities cannot be integrated so easily. The problem with the Muslim communities—and I always use the word in the plural form—was that the nationalist project did not evolve a strategy that could accommodate them.

Don't we also have to imagine how to get beyond this communitarian perspective, in order to reach full integration one day?
MH: We should not seek to achieve that impossible degree of integration, which is what a lot of people were talking about in the 1920s and 1930s. I think we should talk more in terms of accommodation, more in terms of a social contract between different linguistic, religious, and regional groups. We need a new blueprint for accommodating various interests.

What if I feel my belonging to the society as a whole is more important than my communal belonging? I can't always represent the community, and be defined by it alone; there must be some area where I am more or less than the community. The notion of a social contract implies an arrangement between individuals and not between groups.
MH: Individuals should define their place in relation to the community, to society, and to the nation. The whole problem arises when communities become homogenized in terms of their mindset, and begin to negotiate with the state, society, and polity as a community. The problem in the context of India is that the British created a community and that community began to

negotiate, first of all with the Congress, then with the British, and the British were more than willing—for their own imperial reasons, particularly during the inter-war years—to give content and standing to the notion of a community in the political and bureaucratic structures. Somewhere along the line, the choices of the individual become extremely important.

How do you see India's ability to prevent communities from becoming homogenous and, pursuing this logic of identities, fighting against one another?
MH: Much really depends on the social and economic development of the country. A society which is able to equitably distribute its resources, howsoever limited they might be, is likely to develop a much stronger foundation; it is likely to have a better rapport with different segments of society. But a society that is backward, whose resources only certain upper class groups or powerful elements garner is likely to create greater dissension and conflict. And, in so vast and diverse a country as India, we have seen the kind of content which these dissension acquire. So the sense of discrimination, the sense of being left out from the power structures becomes increasingly accentuated. We need an egalitarian society in the true sense of the word, which would ensure that the access to resources is not limited. This means facing not only communities but above all class, which is a daunting task, but obviously one which has to be performed. My argument has always been that Indian society has functioned on a supra-communal basis, more so in rural areas but also significantly enough in urban areas. We need to strengthen these networks. In a growing economy, you would find more and more people relying upon each other, on their mutual expertise, and bridging the gulf that exists in certain parts of the country. Because of the slow progress of the Indian economy, there has been a rupture within the inter-community economic networks; once the economy expands, this gulf can be breached in very significant ways.

How do you respond to your critics who accuse you of making it sound as if it were all the fault of the British?
MH: If you are writing on modern Indian history and are insensitive to the role of colonialism, how can you write about modern India? I don't buy the crude divide-and-rule-policy theory, and yet I do believe that the colonial narrative and its translation into political arrangements lie at the heart of many important explanations. So it is not an orientalist view that I am putting forward; after all, the colonialist discourse was also internalized by a lot of Indians, Muslims and Hindus alike. But I also feel there is merit in the

orientalist discourse, because it does establish the connection between knowledge and power. Today in India, textbooks are being rewritten at the school and college levels: knowledge is being tampered with. Why? The reason is that the protagonists of Hindutva, now holding the reins of power, want to nurture a particularist world-view that is divisive. There is an organized attempt to repudiate the Nehruvian vision that was liberal, modern, and secular. This is, to say the least, an ominous development.

You have argued that the Muslim community in India was partly homogenized by the first Balkan Wars at the beginning of the twentieth century. Did the Balkan Wars of the 1990s have a similar effect?

MH: To some degree, they fostered Islamic solidarity—there is no question about that. But nothing like at the beginning of the twentieth century, when it was orchestrated very effectively by the country's pan-Islamic leaders, who, ironically enough, took sides with the Turks, although Turkey was a colonizing power in the Balkans. And in fact, there were strong movements within Turkey against the Sultan and the Califa. But, there is another dimension to that support, and that is a very powerful anti-colonial sentiment—which Gandhi was able to exploit. Pan-Islamism is the greatest fiction that has been perpetuated for more than a century. We, as scholars, need to provide a corrective to it and Muslim societies need to act in such a way that it is shown to be a shibboleth rather than anything tangible and meaningful.

You have claimed that the nationalisms in both India and Pakistan have failed, and that the dream of Muslim homogeneity has also failed. You have explained the failure of nationalism in India. Could we now go back to Pakistan and try to see how this failure came about and what it implies for contemporary Islam?

MH: Some leaders orchestrated the pan-Islamic movement, aided and abetted by the British government. It petered out in the mid-1920s. Today, Indian Muslims are anguished by what is happening to the Palestinians. They are angry with the West for letting Israel pursue its belligerent policies against Palestine. They are angry with the Arabs, especially the governments, for letting down the Palestinians. I am sure the Pakistanis feel equally agonized. But let me reiterate that Pakistan is caught up in its Islamic rhetoric. That is not conducive to creating a modern nation-state. A modern nation-state cannot be created on the principles of Hindu or Muslim solidarity. Soon after the creation of Pakistan, there developed a strong conflict between the protagonists of modernity and traditionalism. That's because the Jamaat-i

Islami developed as a very major political force. Pakistan took nearly eleven years to draft a constitution because there were such hotly contested visions. These contested visions were an important feature of the nation-building exercise—there was never any consensus on creating a secular society. Thus, as early as 1953, the Ahmadias were targeted, and the Jamaat-i Islami instigated sectarian violence. I think the absence of democratic forces in Pakistani society lies at the heart of any explanation of the disintegration of Pakistan in 1971—I mean the succession of Bangladesh—as well as the current turmoil.

Do you see Partition as a single on-going process?
MI I: I do not think the resurgence of Hindutva in India or Islamic funda-mentalism in Pakistan, is the unfinished agenda of Partition. However, even after fifty-three years, Partition continues to cast its shadow over many aspects of our contemporary life and politics. In that sense, Partition remains an important signpost, an important milestone. At the same time, new groups in India are emerging who want to benefit from globalization, build their own social networks, develop trade and commercial linkages, and create for themselves a better standard of living. Pakistan is, on the other hand, caught up in its search for an identity—an identity that it sometimes defines in relation to west Asia, sometimes in relation to central Asia. What is sad about Pakistan—what is tragic about Muslim society generally—is the absence of any critiques emerging from those societies. What you find are rebuttals—sometimes powerful rebuttals of Western critiques of Muslim societies and Islam. But, at the end of the day, such polemical exchanges do not help the social and economic reconstruction of these societies. In order to hasten the social and economic construction of Muslim societies, what are needed are internal, intellectual critiques, covering both the present and the past.

In that case, it can only stem from the reform of Islam?
MH: The intellectual inertia that has gripped most Muslim societies has to be broken by breaching the citadels of orthodoxy. Muslim societies and intellectuals have to develop a critique outside the conventional formats or platforms made available to them. Unless and until this is done, these societies will continue to be undemocratic, discriminate against women, treat the minorities as inferior, and remain ill-equipped to cope with the challenges of this millennium.

From the Nation to Partition; Through Partition to the Nation

Readings

RADA IVEKOVIĆ

It is unwise to win.

> Jean-François Lyotard, in Jean-François Lyotard and
> Jean-Loup Thébaud, *Au juste* (Paris: Bourgois, 1979)

Those whom domination deprives of ownership are those who will soon have nothing left other than the consolation of belonging. Belonging is the subterfuge by means of which domination will soon convince all those who have nothing left that this nothing is what they own indefeasibly: blood (pure), a name (their own) and a country (the motherland).

> Michel Surya, *De la domination* (Tours: Farrago, 2000)

'The political programme of creating the two nations of India and Pakistan was inscribed upon the bodies of women', says Veena Das. In support of this statement she quotes a number of personal histories, adding:

These cases tend to show that whereas community practices with regard to marriage, adoption and the fostering of children were, at the level of practical kinship, flexible enough to accommodate a wide variety of behaviour, the state's more abstract conception of purity and honour brought women under a far stricter control than that exercised by the family.[1]

The logic of partition means that one arrives at totality and

* Translated from the French by John Doherty

The full-size article is published in French by the Europe and the Balkans International Network: Bologna, Longo Editore: Ravenna. 2001, as 'Occasional Paper' No. 18.

commensurateness with oneself by separation from another self who, at a certain point (where things are teetering on the brink, and war becomes possible), begins to be looked upon as a stranger. One also arrives at this point via the principle of self-determination, which is ambiguous, because it is limited by other possible autonomies.[2] Individual identity is then redefined, and the 'foreign' body is expelled or, on the contrary, the body that properly belongs is reintegrated, and the 'graft' is proclaimed to have been a failure. Common history (which is easier to wipe out than to construct) is then obliterated from memory, and is declared to be that of suffering, that of the 'dark years' (godine mraka, in Serbia as well as in Croatia; for example, due to the 'subjection to others' during the previous regime). The common past is repudiated as a time of oppression in which 'we' were simply innocent victims of the wicked 'others' (and never active protagonists). One thus reinforces non-citizenship; the content of citizenship being, in any case, national,[3] both in the past, because 'not free', and in the present, because of the 'passivization' of individuality and political initiative in homogenization. One then proceeds to the reconstitution of all power relationships, starting with the 'archetypal' hierarchy of the sexes. It has to be seen that this reshaping of the relationships of force and power (which are based on patriarchal hegemony) takes place at all levels, from the intimate and private spheres to the national, state, and trans-state levels.[4] At the same time, the universality preached by the state does not apply to the different dominated parties, other than to subordinate them (the universal itself being a hierarchy). To quote Martine Spensky: 'Up to recent times, modern democratic states, despite the universalist principle that founded them, were able to separate out certain 'national' groups within the purview of the law itself, without seeing in this any contradiction with their founding principle.'[5] But the same is true of the nation, whose universalist claim stops at its borders, and is limited to its nationals, given that the universal establishes its secularized divine scope (which consists of including 'everyone'), and a relationship to the infinite that is expressed, precisely, in a hierarchy, and thus, paradoxically, in a system of inclusions and exclusions which are at once complementary and gradual. In other words, the universal can only come into its own through the subordinated inclusion of the particular. As in a tribe, or a religion, we recognize ourselves as members of the same species, and as participants in the universal, only by reference to a higher authority, and thus, paradoxically, by accepting the given order in advance. It is in unity as such that a basis for partition is to be found.

Of course, partitions are linked to the setting up of nation-states, making the nation a captive of the state.[6] It is true that the state, as well as the nation, excludes some people. And, as Marie-Claire Caloz-Tschopp puts it very well in her book on stateless people, which is of considerable current interest, 'the national/non-national has become a fundamental discriminating category, an indicator of the dominant conception of the political community and its principle of cohesion and exclusion, which has been implemented in the space of a closed, hierarchicalized, divided state territory. The non-national and the national are in effect defined only in relation to the nation-state. The globalization of the system of nation-states in the terrestrial physical space and the public space has led to the disappearance of the state as heir [to the protective function].'[7] Today it is obvious that the nation-state itself is what gives rise to one of our major evils: the stateless, the 'superfluous', the deported, the displaced, the refugees; and all this on the basis of its principles of sovereignty and self-determination, pushed to an extreme point. The nation secretes its margins—those of the 'marginal nation'.[8] And the nation thus marginalized is the product of an emergent nation: there is no centre without a periphery. After the fall of the Yugoslav nation (a nation that was undeclared, never named, and thus non-existent), marginal nations were born on its edges, which tended to recentre. But when there is a lot of uncertainty about a nation, populations can push other identities to the forefront, in a life that crosses borders—borders which are in any case in a constant state of reconfiguration.[9] And, to digress for a moment (though in fact it is hardly a digression at all), we might emphasize the obscure connection that can exist between sovereignty (self-determination), the fact of being centred on oneself (whether as an individual or a group, an institution or a state), the principle of identity and continuity, and the imperative of domination and violence,[10] while at the same time all of them are also forms of resistance to being crushed by outside forces: by sovereignty, domination, and violence against other people. And, just as the human being is born in an incomplete state, incapable of autonomy, the nation too has an incomplete appearance, and wears itself out trying to compensate for this shortcoming.

The Indian sub-continent was divided, in blood, in 1947. Two countries—India and Pakistan—acceded to independence in and through civil war. For fifty years, the exaltation of independence masked the original violence.[11] Pakistan was founded on a religious basis, whereas India, in principle, was founded on a secular basis. In 1971, Bangladesh was born out of a continuation of this division, and the consequent rifts that took place within the sub-continent are still present. The Kashmir war is chronic.[12] From the time of the anti-colonialist war, the future Pakistan, in its quest for independence, promulgated the so-called theory of the 'two nations' (Muslim and Hindu), which India officially rejected. As an irony of history would have it, this theory, which did not match up with reality at the outset, has become true over the course of the last half-century, in the sense that the nation is, in any case, a construction.[13] But the two (and more) emergent nations have not been divided up exactly in the way that was envisaged at the time by the separatists of the Muslim League, given that the Indian Muslims either chose to affiliate to the Indian nation or just happened to be there anyway.[14] And in partition as a continuous process, this initial difference meant that the discourse of separation, and implicitly that of exclusion, became officialized (statist and foundationalist) in Pakistan, sometimes in a glorified form; which fostered the temptation to fundamentalism, and even led to subsequent support for the neighbouring Taliban, inspired by the United States' cold-war policy, and that of Saudi Arabia. And India—where fragmentation both on the borders and inside them, along with inter-community violence, have grown in scale since the 'birth of the nation'[15]— has not been exempt from comparable after-effects. 'The structure of communal authority', as Partha Chatterjee writes, 'must be located primarily in the domain of ideology.'[16] It can then organize violence.

In India, the theme of partition has remained almost taboo (except in official versions) for fifty years, and it is still a delicate subject in Pakistan. It has been overshadowed by discussions about the liberation process, and the creation of the nation, in the context of colonialism. Partition, and especially the accompanying violence that is perpetrated everywhere, has been the price of independence, and is thus passed over in silence.[17]

Alternative accounts then begin to come up where they were not expected, especially through the work of historians who, starting with a particular symptom, would unveil a subject that had been above scrutiny up till then, while also making it accessible to many more potentially interested parties. This was the case with the opening up of discussion—especially by women, and for women's benefit—about the history of the partition of India (which in fact was to become multipartitioned) fifty years after the events in question (with the work of R. Menon, U. Butalia, V. Das, and others). For official India, and especially for the nationalist Hindus, the guilty party was still the Muslim League and the theory of the two nations; for official

Pakistan, it was Hindu nationalism.[18] It was a partition that came through in the national discourse, structured exactly as we have just described it, and which proscribed the expression of other subjects, options or issues. Given that the nation is a community born out of partition (and that it is not-all, even in its claim to completeness), every community that is subordinated to it (as all of them are) can only follow the same example. In fact, a community is constructed out of more or less brutal exclusion. But the fully-constituted nation-state, having been established through violence, then claims it will put an end to all violence in the future.

Secularism Under Threat

During and since partition, India has been officially secular, but this secularism is constantly being eroded and threatened by the 'neutral', particularist 'universalism' of its Hindu majority, whose fundamentalist inclinations are becoming more and more perceptible.[19] One important detail: religion and the state have different, though comparable, ways of setting up patriarchal hierarchies, and share a complaisant complicity with respect to women.[20] Today, inter-community violence (ethnic or religious) is widespread, but there is still a refusal to see its origin in the constitution of the nation as such, one of whose major instruments is the great patriarchal share-out. R. Samaddar remarks that ethnicity is supposed to vandalize a nation, whereas democracy sanctifies it, and the status of democracy is denied to ethnic groups which claim to adhere to the principle. On what basis? Where can one find a basis for making distinctions between ethnicity and the nation, if not in the terms themselves? And Samaddar replies, while insisting on the pragmatic criterion that is centred on oneself: 'Thus nation for me, ethnicity for you;[21] likewise we are going global, you are getting fragmented; ours is democracy, yours is violence; we are sovereign and therefore we can contract treaties, your locus is subordinate, so you can have accords.'[22] What is constantly reproduced in this way, he says later on, is the outsider of the nation, who is necessary to its authentification. There is no nation without enemies.[23] Negotiations and peace agreements generally sanction a de facto state of affairs, along with divisions that have already taken place, which are themselves the result of conflict.[24]

Colonialism left India with a heritage of different civil codes for the different religious communities, which is the distinguishing feature of Indian secularism. The condition of women remains, even now, to a large extent

governed by these irreducible legal differences. Communities are distinguished from one another through the 'private' way in which each of them
treats women. As is always the case in the construction of a nation, the
control of women is a major issue, but 'the juridical domain in which the
social reformers were constructing womanhood was not very different to
personal laws based on religious scriptures. Therefore the so-called champi-
oning of women's freedom in the agitation of the social reformers should be
re-examined', writes Jashodhara Bagchi.[25] This type of history has been
repeated since the birth of the independence movement. The manipulation
of constructed otherness is at the basis of the constitution of the national
and/or religious identity. The blurred lines between religious and national
identity were deliberate, permitting shadings into, and legitimations by,
other fields. And when Christophe Jaffrelot talks about Hindu 'nationalism'
rather than 'fundamentalism', he is no doubt right.[26]

The complex work done by the latter author also gives an up-to-date
account of the relationship between the construction of these identities in
the subcontinent, the political and public field, and the state form. The
recent growing politicization of the castes—their changes of function, for
example, and their new forms of association, and then federation, through
which they play a part in political activities—is remarkably described in
L'Inde contemporaine de 1950 à nos jours, up to the new surge forward by the
'untouchables' and the dalits.[27] This had the effect of sharpening the conflict
with the nationalist Hindus, and it was also a sort of riposte aimed at them.
Les nationalistes hindous is a collection which makes implicit, if not explicit,
the relationship that exists between partition and nationalism (Hindu, in
this case), while the two books on Pakistan by the same author examine the
relationship between the 'origin-based' violence of secession and the internal
('ethnic') and regional tensions which already existed. Torn apart by this
'origin-based sin', present-day Pakistan still seems to be in search of a real
identity, while lying primarily at the intersection of strategic currents flowing
from the Middle East, Southern Asia and Central Asia (Transcaucasia,
Afghanistan), and China. Its low level of national integration is due, among
other things, to numerous conflicts between the 'ethnic' communities, and
between 'majority' and 'minority' groups in the regions; hence the tendency,
on the part of the oligarchy, to promote an Islamization that is ever more
important as an instrument of unification. 'This difference between majority
and minority can largely be explained by the almost federal political system
that characterized British India. The Muslim elite of the united provinces,

and that of the presidency of Bombay, wanted to get back a state that they could govern (and this was also the case for the Muslim military), or a market for their businesses, while those of the regions that had Muslim majorities were already in power, and had nothing to fear from the Hindus.'[28] We have seen this same desire for a state elsewhere, for example in ex-Yugoslavia, where it was multiplied by a factor of eight (six republics and two autonomous regions). The low level of integration also resulted from the fact that Pakistan seemed incapable of building stable institutions. And if religion does not really seem to be a sufficient condition for the creation of an integrated nation, Pakistan does still exist as the nightmare of its brother-enemy, India, due to, among other things, its highly unstable military regime, which possesses the atom bomb.[29] Integration, while remaining incomplete (but is it not the case that every nation, every state, is in the same situation, by definition?), still continues to advance.[30]

Ch. Jaffrelot's writings deal with the different countries of the sub-continent, essentially since the liberation period. Hindu nationalism (like the *varna* system and that of the castes, though in a different way) represents an attempt to transcend the differences and divisions in conditions which are not brought together by a great tradition[31] (monotheist, we might add). And this is perhaps the reason why nationalism chose to follow the 'religious sect' model rather than that of traditional social stratifications (imaginary or real), or an approach which, at first glance, would have been clearly identified as political.[32] Thus, for the nationalists, the model of the nation is precisely that of the (religious) community. In India, the central issue here, following the struggle for independence, lies in the balance of forces between Hindu nationalism and Indian nationalism, represented at the time of liberation by the secularism of the Congress Party, and by Nehru himself.[33] The de-legitimation of this Nehru-inspired, secular model of the state and society began to be accentuated in the 1980s,[34] in spite of the important role played by culture in the preservation of national unity, and this tendency joined up with the nationalist Hindu current, whose origins went back to the middle of the nineteenth century (but also to the quarrel over Ayodhya, which reached its apogee in 1992 when the mosque there was destroyed in favour of the temple). Though this was not predestined, and in the absence of any new project, the erosion of Indian secularism was hastened, on the one hand, by Indira Gandhi's repression and, on the other hand, by the political exploita-tion of religious cleavages, both of which militated against a more substantial form of democracy. And here we might add that this period of discomfiture of the secular project (which was that of the initial decolonization period) ended up in the globalist framework at the same time that the cold war was ending and 'real socialism' was disappearing, at least in Europe, spurred on by a similar resistance to democratization on the part of the various oligarchies which, in both contexts, attempted to preserve their privileges by adopting a nationalist type of discourse. This convergence appears to us to be significant, and not at all fortuitous: it would seem to be a case of a global process.[35] Integration on the world scale produces a fragmentation of identity (ethnicist, culturalist or religious, it matters little) on the local level. At this scale, the name one adopts[36] and the form in which one imagines oneself are very important.

The terms (the language) chosen for the official denomination of a nation determine its comprehension. The Indian union—a composite state—considers that only the whole can be considered as the nation. The error of analysis in India, which was deliberate in that it was due to a concern for the independence and construction of the national state, as well as a nation-society, was that it failed to see the identity between the structure and functioning of the nation and the community. This made it possible to conceal the fact that the same logic of violence was behind both, and that it could not but come out as soon as it was legitimized by raison d'état and independence. At the time of its appearance, and before it is historically—and by the will (or with the consent) of the citizen body-built up into a society (which is not a foregone conclusion), the nation is simply a community with a vertical hierarchy. It is essentially non-democratic towards everything it excludes, practising a form of 'democracy' limited to its own people. In this uncertain process of becoming a nation-society, which is always possible but never guaranteed in advance, the subject must still become a citizen, emancipating him/herself individually from his/her subjection to the community. One is Indian individually, not as a member of a community. The terms were much less clear in Yugoslavia, and this contributed to a general confusion of identity.[37] Paradoxically, the community had to transform itself in depth into a dynamic, open structure in order to constitute a society through adjudicating between the positions of the different parties involved. But in the promise and the nomination of the nation (-society), there was the presence of democracy, and narrative anticipation gave the impression that this was already at hand. In other words, the nation-community lent credence to a nation-society that did not yet exist.[38] One can thus formally separate out, as though they were mutually opposed, the different communities (perceived as religious rather than ethnic) and the Indian nation as such. 'Any consideration of the nationstate must reflect on the question of nations that are incorporated into larger political formations', writes Ravinder Kumar. 'The classic example of this phenomenon was the USSR, which, in theory at least, was made up of a certain number of nations combined into a federation, which protected their cultural identity while at the same time reinforcing their participation in a broader federal community. India (...) is another example of this type. It is made up of a certain number of well-defined linguistic and cultural units called states, which have been assembled into a republic in which the power and authority of the centre are foregrounded to the detriment of the power and authority of the constitutive states. The Soviet Union has been formally described as a multi-national community in which each republic represented a quite distinct nation within the huge federation. The Indian republic, on the other hand, has been formally defined as a single nation composed of a constellation of sub-nationalities, each forming a state within the nation.'[39]

The Yugoslav Counter-example

The foregoing is exactly the opposite of the situation in Yugoslavia between 1945 and 1990, where there was a more or less unofficial[40] ban on the designation and the concept of a pan-Yugoslav nation, so as not to offend the national and identity-based sensitivities of the different parties concerned, and in the name of a multinational federation of citizens.[41] One good reason for this refusal to create a Yugoslav nation lay in the founding fathers' desire not to foster a form of greater-Serbian nationalism disguised as Yugoslavianism, which was a real threat.[42] Between 1945 and 1991, officially, Yugoslavia was multi-national and multi-cultural. From the viewpoint of the Indians, the fact of belonging to the different states of the union did not necessarily entail any identity in terms of nationality or citizenship of the federal units. The retreat into identity was not based on regional origins (or at any rate only to a small extent, and in some cases late in the day), but rather on religion and custom, in other words 'culture' (in an a-territorial sense, which brought it all the closer to essentialism). But it was inscribed in, and started with, the birth of the nation. The Indian union always takes precedence over membership of the different states, whereas Yugoslavia became highly decentralized over the course of time. The inhabitants of a member-state of the Union do not have its nationality, such as this was constructed in ex-Yugoslavia. There are no nation-states within India (which is in itself a nation-state), as there were within socialist Yugoslavia, where each republic was a nation-state (with the original exception of Bosnia-Herzegovina, which was 'tri-national'). In India, 'political affectivity' and identity have to do with membership of a more or less religious community, a language, the immediate and the familiar, the region, without reference to any structural political organization. In any case, linguistic, cultural, and communal identities are not always geographical or territorial. Identities, and even nationality, are more open, and borders are unofficially more flexible, or indeed impossible to control.[43] Communities whose origins are in a particular part of the country can live indefinitely in a distant region, while retaining their specific way of life. Some towns are very cosmopolitan, in a sub-continental way.[44] Communities speaking different languages have always existed, as have highly diversified classes (though the hierarchy according to which they are organized is another question).

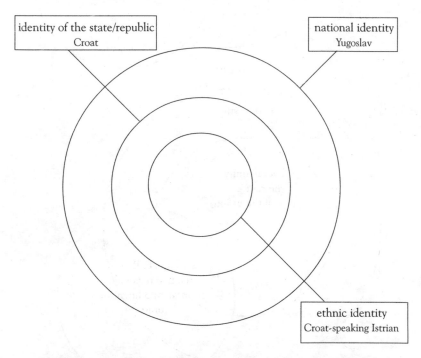

identity of the state/republic
Croat

national identity
Yugoslav

ethnic identity
Croat-speaking Istrian

Fig. 1: Graphic representation of the inclusive model of multiple identities: local ethnic identity spreads through different types of identification, up to national identity.[45]

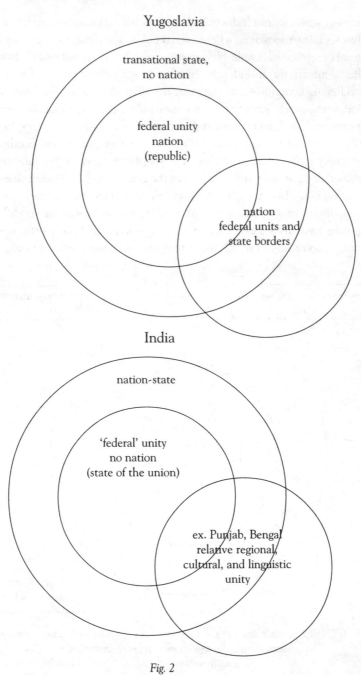

Fig. 2

In both cases, fragmentation becomes visible in the inner circle, but it originates in the outer circle.

Yugoslavia	India
Nationalism: negative	Nationalism: positive
Civic patriotism for the federation which represents the totality	Nationalism: patriotism for the totality
Nationalism = fragmentation	Nationalism = unity
Nationalism = communalism	Nationalism versus communalism
The transnational is everything	The nation is everything
The totality is not monolithic	The nation is monolithic
Differences are (quite) important and represented officially (ritually)	Differences are not a part of the political definition, but are recognized
'Fraternity and unity' (no sisters admitted)	'Unity in diversity' (no sexes recognized)
Secularism and religious differences (unimportant)	Secularism, plus the hegemony of religious differences

In Yugoslavia, the shaping of the different nationalisms followed the lines of the federal units,[46] along with Serbian trans-territorial specificity, and a similar Croatian extra-territorial aspiration in Herzegovina (with trans-territoriality being tacitly proclaimed by nationalists on both sides, and reactivated at the time of the break-up). It was a question of the relationship between the centre and the states. What prevented the formal expression of pluralism in Yugoslavia was the single party-state and democracy without parties, expressed as self-management.[47] The real pluralism of ideas which did actually exist within the party (though these ideas were not articulated, systematized or authorised in the 'raw' state) was no more than a relatively vague ideological construct. In principle it was subjected to the higher interests of the political class that had to be defended, with a dogmatic façade and a show of unity that were deemed to be untouchable. In India, plurality can be freely expressed 'as long as it does not call into question the unity of the nation'.[48] In Yugoslavia, it could be expressed as long as it did not oppose the interests of the regime and the ruling powers; it being assumed— wrongly—that unity had been acquired once and for all. The centre was able to manoeuvre and make concessions in both cases, but the issues were not the same. The centre, in Yugoslavia, was the party (the party-state), which, paradoxically, had to accommodate to a substantial degree of administrative and territorial decentralization.[49] But in India, the centre is the state; and if, in general, the state units have no national identity, there are nonetheless instances of communalism, even if they are not always territorially determined.[50] And some, like that of the Punjab, have in fact constantly changed their principle of division in their quest for adaptation. The term 'communalism' is an example of a very Indian use of English. It is applied both to caste as such and to the community of castes; to religion, also, but always in the patriarchal, vertical sense of the term, which excludes society, along with its public and political space. Caste, for its part, is a community based on birth. It is fundamentally exclusive, organized round the idea of ritual purity, and in complex interaction with other groups and criteria. This system is dynamic and in constant adjustment, contrary to how it may appear. Caste is determined by the hierarchy of the sexes, and by imaginary racial 'purity', that is, by the obsession of origins and the principle of the maintenance of identity.[51] It is highly sexuated, and the hierarchy of the sexes regulates other inequalities. But castes are far from being the only reality of Indian society, and they have much more complex functions of differentiation and integration than simply those of separation which have generally been attributed to them in the West. Their very hierarchy is marked by a claim to universality.[52] The castes integrate through hierarchy, through top-down favouritism, and through their interdependence in practical terms.[53]

Divisionist or Secessionist

Urvashi Butalia has accurately grasped the nature of the relationship between the dislocation of the country and the different forms of social disintegration in this regime of castes and classes.[54] Rejection and exclusion are complementary, support each other, and are mutually reinforcing, with the result that they legitimize each other. In the marginalization to which they are subjected, women, pariahs, communalists, the different casteless people, the other religions, the farmers, and so on, bear witness to the apartheid and patriarchies that operate at every level (though of course this is in no way an exclusively Indian phenomenon). Such elements give an edge to Butalia's writing, which, like other remarkable contributions to the unrivalled series of documents and exposées that have been appearing in recent years, is made up of examples, collected narratives, and direct history, as recounted by the protagonists in, and the victims of, the events in question.

The entity as a whole (India, the nation) has always been fragile, because it was flawed right from the start; but at the same time it has never been contested by political language, except marginally. However, this divisionist marginality exemplifies the secessionist nature of the nation itself, which is always either already divided up or else in the process of coming into being. This is the opposite of what happened in Yugoslavia, where partition also took place, giving an example to follow. In India, the concept of a nation and its verbal expression were reserved for the entity as a whole (a union of states, India in its entirety), and for each person's identity (individually, but also in common and with reference to the society) as a citizen of the nation. In Yugoslavia, on the contrary, the status of the nation(s) was not clarified. This status was not officially the opposite of that of the Indian nation, that is, the nation was not seen as deriving from the community, as 'something pre-political'. It was, strictly speaking, seen as being decreed from above in an abstract way, and by a 'divine' will. Its constructed character was surreptitiously accepted, if only by the care that the rulers took not to put together any Yugoslav nation as such. But the nation was not based on the individual, any more than on the community. It was as though there had been a desire to define the community otherwise, for example as a self-managed community composed of aware self-managers (who in other respects were supposed to be 'neutral'). But the imaginary, desired 'entirety' of India was a paradox in the sense that, in and through partition, the nation recognized itself as non-entire. The differences concerned only regional or communal identities, and did not undermine the universal. This, and the nation, were presented only at the beginning as being obscure in their unfinished, and unfinishable, character. They were postulated 'as (a) whole', a promise to be honoured at the price of future partitions. In India, the maintenance of the fiction of totality was made possible, among other factors, by the existence of a large, strong, pan-Indian middle class which was up to the task. It was a vehicle for Indian cultural integration, in the same way that it is now the agent of the country's new liberalist prosperity. This culture, and these common interests (with all their diversities), represent a real reservoir of pan-Indian integration which originated in continuity.[55] It does not simply suffer from the weakness of Yugoslav symbolic (in the sense of 'imaginary') capitalism,[56] or that of romanticized socialist multi-culturalism, and is in no way a mere symbolic surrogate. This common cultural reservoir can be used in a genuine way, in that it produces a form of tangible common heritage, and is, not simply a cosmetic way of filling quotas, as was the case in Yugoslavia in the sphere of official culture due to a lack of social and cultural integration. In India, this heritage can only be weakened by communal splits (which indeed are not in short supply). But there is a good chance that it will survive for a long time yet on the strength of assets that are valid for a non-negligible proportion of the population, that is, the privileged, and the middle classes— and given also the quantity (dimension) involved, in absolute terms—and not just on the basis of purely symbolic claims, though indeed the symbolism is real enough in itself.

Ambiguous Modernity

Since the struggle for independence, in India as in other formerly-colonized countries, nationalism has been a positive, liberating concept: it is the one that was destined to bring about the interlocking independence of the nation and the state, the nation being at the service of the state.[57] Nationalism, as an emancipating force whose spirit of resistance was forged during the long colonial period, is ambiguous about the differences between the sexes. And it is important to be clear about this, because the hierarchy of the sexes tends to present itself as archetypal, in the sense that it underlies and determines all the other hierarchies in its role of supervising 'racial purity'. The control of sexuality is a very persuasive means of coercion in any framework what-ever, and it takes precedence over the state.[58] It is the colony that brings to fruition and sets up the state which is later to become independent. The colony brings about an ambiguous, displaced form of modernity that is supposed to be applied to 'pre-modern' conditions. It thus produces results that are politically, socially, and culturally different from those to be found in the West. The colonizers are members of societies which like to think of themselves as democratic and universalist (but which do not apply these principles in the territories they occupy).[59] All of this has the effect of expelling the subject from his/her traditional community, thus inducing the latter to attempt a reformulation of social ties (which is always based on a reconstitution and adjustment of the patriarchate). This can take place either through a more or less conservative or obscurantist 're-traditionalization' (recommunalization), or through an attempt on the part of the subject to make a 'free' choice within the society (a more modern, conflict-ridden choice, and possibly, at most, the outline of a modern patriarchal society). Communalist modes of distribution of power can very well co-exist with a statist—or even a modern—mode of organization of power, so that the two do not take place on the same level, but rather intersect.[60] With the state, however, there is also the separation of private and public power; and it is here that one gets a direct glimpse of the fact that 'power is naked', and that 'the universal is empty'. Henceforth, the father is only the head of the family, wielding more or less arbitrary individual power in the home, whereas for the colonial state he may be the enemy, the subaltern, the dissident, and so on. Colonialism weakens this 'local' father. And so the father, who in principle is a figure of domination, takes revenge on his dependents; for example, he can re-establish the hierarchy by attaching his personal power to that of a resistance movement, which thereby becomes an accomplice of oppression by the family, the caste, and the community. Liberation on one front does not automatically mean liberation on another front, and, according to the circumstances, it can take on ever-new configurations. J. Habermas seems to be unaware of the ambivalence of this conditional, transplanted modernity (which is nonetheless a force for liberation, however incompletely, in non-European contexts) when, buoyed up with optimism, he talks about the social reconfiguration that takes place 'with each advance': 'With each new advance in modernization, intersubjectively-experienced worlds open up, reorganize themselves and close down again. This change in form is at the heart of classical sociology, which gives ever-new descriptions of the phenomenon: from status to contract, from the primary group to the secondary group, from community to society, from mechanical solidarity to organic solidarity, etc. The impulse to open up comes from new markets, new resources, new lines of communication.'[61]

In this way one perceives, among other things, that in national liberation struggles there is a double control which is exercised over women, and that this is instrumental in the reconfiguration of power, 'first by the male of one community who establishes his own 'identity' by exercizing his territoriality over her body, second by her 'own' community which talks about compulsions of ritual purity so as to exclude her from the ritually pure domains of hearth and marriage, and drinking water.'[62] The 'vacuum' of power, or of the universal, is immediately 'filled' by the concrete demands of political immediacy.[63] The missing link in the explanation of the Yugoslavian rout is not nationalism, but rather the alternatives and resistances to it which have been passed over in silence.[64] As R. Samaddar says, in another context, 'the history of the partition of India remains incomplete without the narrative of how this history is built upon silencing the counter voices.'[65]

As long as India continues to act as a general framework for all its different peoples, the term 'nationalism' will retain its positive connotation. By tacit convention, it does not apply to the different separatisms or autonomisms (and they are numerous) that are to be found in India, especially in the border regions. In ex-Yugoslavia, on the other hand, liberation from Second-World-War fascism did not take place under a uni-national banner, but started with a common, popular 'front' of the different peoples and, subsequently, a coalition of all concerned within a community of republics in a federal unification process which in theory could have elicited a 'citizens' patriotism', but never one of an ethnic, national, or religious type. And within this putative 'citizens' patriotism', which in reality was never achieved, an excess of respect for nations, due to a concern with achieving a balance between all of them, accompanied by a fear of sanctioning majority nationalism, precipitated the nation into purely personal ways of thinking, without any status in terms of citizenship. But it was the absence of an integrated society, democracy, and political articulation (as well as a particular combination of circumstances), rather than a surfeit of nations, that sealed the fate of Yugoslavia and, what was worse, led to war.

Notes

1. Veena Das, *Critical Events: An Anthropological Perspective on Contemporary India* (Delhi: Oxford University Press, 1999), pp. 56 and 81.

2. Immanuel Wallerstein, *After Liberalism* (New York: The New Press, 1995).

3. M. Spensky (ed.), *Universalisme, particularisme et citoyennete dans les îles Britanniques* (Paris: L'Harmattan, 2000), p. 17. Citizenship itself has two faces, autonomy, of course, but also 'voluntary' submission to a state and a nation. As E. Hobsbawm says, this was what gave rise to the conscript armies of the past. See A. Polito (ed.), *Intervista sul nuovo secolo* (Bari: Laterza, 1999), p. 32.

4. These complementary reclassifications do not, however, necessarily take place in the same way, or at the same pace, in all the different registers. The different 'patriarchies' can have a certain autonomy, and a different periodicity from the other inequalities that they underlie. See Kumkum Sangari and Sudesh Vaid. 'Recasting Women: An Introduction', in K. Sangari and S. Vaid (eds), *Recasting Women: Essays in Indian Colonial History* (New Brunswick, N.J.: Rutgers University Press. 1990), p. 5.

5. M. Spensky, op. cit., p. 13.

6. For the concept of the nation as a captive of the state. see Alain Touraine. *Comment sortir du libéralisme?* (Paris: Fayard, 2000).

7. M.-C. Caloz-Tschopp, *Les sans-Etat dans la philosophie d'Hannah Arendt* (Lausanne: Payot 2000), pp. 203–4.

8. As far as Umberto Melotti is concerned, contemporary migrations are also producing the new racism. *Migrazioni, nazionalità, cittadinanza. Sui pregiudizi e sul razzismo* (Rome: Il Mondo 3 Edizioni, 1996).

9. R. Samaddar, *The Marginal Nation Transborder Migration from Bangladesh to West Bengal* (New Delhi/London/Thousand Oaks: Sage Publications, 1999). For another concrete example, see R. Samaddar, 'Nagaland's past in the crystal ball', in *The Telegraph*, 17 November 1999.

10. Etienne Balibar, *La Crainte des masses* (Paris: Galilée, 1997): Alain Brossat, *Le corps de l'ennemi. Hyperviolence et démocratie* (Paris: la Fabrique, 1998); Jacques Derrida, 'Pulsion de mort, cruauté et psychanalyse', in *Le Monde*, 9–10 July 2000; Klaus Theweleit, ONE + ONE (Berlin: Brinkmann and Bose, 1995); *Un plus un, Memory pictures, suiride One + One* (Paris: Théâtre Typographique, 2000).

11. See, among others: Urvashi Butalia, *The Other Side of Silence. Voices from the Partition of India* (New Delhi: Viking, 1998); Veena Das, *Critical Events: An Anthropological Perspective in Contemporary India* (Delhi: Oxford University Press, 1995); Mushirul Hasan, *Legacy of a Divided Nation: India's Muslims since Independence* (Oxford University Press India, 1997): Mushirul Hasan (ed.), *India Partitioned. The Other Face of Freedom* 1947–1997, Vols 1 and 2, 1995,1997; M. Hasan, 'Memories of a Fragmented Nation: rewriting the histories of India's partition', in *Economic and Political Weekly*, No. 33 (41), October 1997; M. Hasan (ed.), *Invented Boundaries—Gender, Politics and the Partition of India* (Delhi: Oxford University Press, 2000); Radha Kumar, *Divide and Fall? Bosnia in the Annals of Partition* (London: Verso, 1998); *Interventions. International Journal of Post-Colonial Studies*, special issue, 'The Partition of the Indian Sub-Continent', Ritu Menon (ed.), Vol. 1, No. 2, 1999; R. Menon and Kamla Bhasin, *Borders & Boundaries. Women in India's Partition* (New Brunswick, N.J: Rutgers University Press, 1998); Ranabir Samaddar (ed.), *Reflexions on the Partition in the East* (Delhi: Vikas, 1997). See also *South Asia Bulletin*, Vol. 7, Nos 1–2, 1987, Vol. 8, Nos 1–2, 1988, Vol. 9, No. 2, 1989, etc. In literature, among others, see Aamer Hussein (ed.), *Hoops of Fire. Fifty Years of Fiction by Pakistani Women* (London. Saqui Books, 1999); Quratulain Hyder, *River of Fire [Aag ka darya]*, Kali for Women (Delhi, 1998). Mani Kapur, *Difficult Daughters* (London: Faber & Faber, 1999); Bhisham Sahni, *Tamas* [Darkness] (New Delhi: Penguin India, 1974).

12. Paula Banerjee , 'The Tenuons Line: The Line of Control in Kashmir', in Ranabir Samaddar and Helmut Reifeld (eds), *Peace as Process: Reconciliation and Conflict Resolution in South Asia* (Delhi: Manohar Publishers, 2001).

13. Benedict Anderson, *Imagined Communities. Reflections on the Origin and Spread of Nationalism* (London/New York: Verso, 1983). Etienne Balibar and Immanuel Wallerstein, *Race nation classe Les identités ambiguës* (Paris: La Découverte, 1990).

14. See the interview with Mushirul Hasan in this issue.

15. The title of a text by R. Samaddar, 'Birth of a Nation', in R. Samaddar (ed.), *Reflections on Partition in the East* (Delhi: Vikas, 1997). In the same way that nations

'are born' (and they are, in fact, 'birth' by definition!), they can commit suicide, as was the case with Yugoslavia.

16. P. Chatterjee, 'More on Modes of power and the Peasantry', in R. Guha and G. Chakravarty Spivak (eds), *Selected Subaltern Studies* (New York/Oxford: Oxford University Press, 1988), p. 382.

17. The same phenomenon has been observed in nationalist, statist Croatia: independence won out over partition, which was seen as liberation exclusively. Atrocities could only, officially (the natianalist officiality of the HDZ party, the 'Croatian democratic community'), be committed by others, never by 'us'. In a way, the victim is morally exonerated in advance, being innocent according to his/her own definition; and any other interpretation is nothing more than an indication of treason and enmity.

18. See Hérodote, No. 71, 'L'Inde et la question nationale', 1993, special issue edited by Jean-Luc Racine; Ch. Jaffrelot (ed.), *Le Pakistan, carrefour de tensions régionales* (Paris: Editions Complexe, 1999), and particularly Jean-Luc Racine, 'Le syndrome indien. Entre Cachemire et nucleaire', pp. 38 ff.; Ch. Jaffrelot (ed.), *Le Pakistan* (Paris: Fayard, 2000). On this subject, see the chapters by Jaffrelot himself and J.-L. Racine.

19. There is much to be said about the particularity of Indian secularism. See the articles in this issue; also, Partha Chatterjee, 'Secularism and Toleration', *in Economic and Political Weekly,* 9 July 1994; Revue de géographie et de géopolitique, in *Hérodote,* No. 71, 1994, special issue, 'L'Inde et la question nationale', Jean-Luc Racine (ed.), articles by J.-L. Racine, Ch. Jaffrelot, and M.J. Zins; Nivedita Menon, 'State/Gender/ Community. Citizenship in Contemporary India', in *Economic and Political Weekly,* Vol. XXXIII, No. 5, January 1998. See also the essays by Amartya Sen on Indian secularism, in various publications, e.g. *Laicismo indiano,* in A. Massarenti (ed.) (Milan: Feltrinelli, 1998). In the end, secularism is not concerned with a separation between state and religion, but with equal treatment for all religions on the part of the state. Secularism also introduces a framework of interpretation, and criteria that are at once modern and Western, according to which only modern, non-communal- ist, non-religious Indians are 'good'. Thus Indian society is split, along with its other cleavages, into 'secularists' and 'irrational communalist obscurantists', and all those who do not identify with the former can only be Hindus, Muslims, Sikhs, etc' not having the option of not explicitly adhering to a religion. 'Secularism and statism go hand in hand in India', concludes Ashis Nandy, in 'Secularism', in *Seminar,* No. 394, June 1992, p. 30, quoted by J.-L. Racine in 'Rama et les joueurs de dés ...' *in L'Inde et la question nationale,* p. 40, note 14. Furthermore, it may be worth recalling, as John Keane does, that at times 'secularism is the refuge of violent intolerance' of Western origin; in 'Les limites du sécularisme', in *Le Bulletin de la Lettre internationale,* No. 14, summer 1999, p. 61.

20. Kumkum Sangari, 'Politics of Diversity. Religious Communities and Multiple

Patriarchies', in *Economic and Political Weekly*, 23 December 1995; Partha Chaterjee, 'The Nationalist Resolution of the Women's Question', in K. Sangari and S. Vaid (eds), *Recasting Women. Essays in Indian Colonial History* (New Brunswick, N.J: Rutgers University Press, 1990).

21. Or, the universal for me and the particular for you: 'In the liberal system, the dominant figures set themselves up as 'universal', and shunt off to the side of the 'particular' those who are excluded, and who organize into specific groups to defend their interests', writes Martine Spensky in 'Universalisme des hommes, particularisme des femmes', in M. Spensky (ed.), *Universalisme, particularisme et citoyenneté dans les Iles Britanniques*. op. cit., pp. 127–8.

22. 'Those Accords. A Bunch of Documents', *South Asia Forum for Human Rights*, Paper Series 4 (Kathmandu, 2000), pp. 4–5.

23. The difference between a 'nation' and an 'ethnic group' is analogous to that between a 'language' and a 'dialect'. It is a question of convention. A language is a dialect that has succeeded politically, and a nation is an ethnic group that has done the same thing.

24. Tanja Sekulić, 'Distruzione etnonazionalista della società. il caso della Bosnia', in Giuseppe Ieraci, Liborio Mattina, *Studi politici*, special issue devoted to Central, Eastern and Balkan Europe (Trieste: EUT, 1999), p. 259.

25. Jashodhara Bagchi, 'Women's Empowerment: Paradigms and Paradoxes', in Uma Chakravarty and Kumkum Sangari (eds), *From Myths to Markets* (New Delhi: Manohar, 1999), p. 373. 'The consolidation of domestic values based on the religious 'personal laws' was one of the forms of construction of the ideology of anti-colonial resistance', writes J. Bagchi in the introduction to J. Bagchi (ed.), *Indian Women: Myth and Reality* (Hyderabad: Sangam Books, 1995), p. 11. The same book contains an interesting text in which Tanika Sarkar analyses the contradiction between the construction by Hindu nationalists of the myth of the woman in ancient India (as being independent and intellectual), and, side by side with this (in the nineteenth century), their celebration of child marriages and patriarchal values. 'Hindu Conjugality and Nationalism in Late Nineteenth Century Bengal', *ibid.*, pp. 98–115.

26. Ch. Jaffrelot, *Les Nationalistes hindous. Idéologie, implantation et mobilisation des années 1920 aux années 1990* (Paris: Presse de la Fondation Nationale des Sciences Politiques, 1993); also, 'Nationalisme hindou, territoire et société', in *Hérodote*, No. 71, 'L' Inde et la question nationale', pp. 93–112.

27. Ch. Jaffrelot (ed.), *L' Inde contemporaine de 1950 à nos jours* (Paris: Fayard, 1996): see the part written by Jackie Assayag, pp 373 ff., 378 ff.

28. Ch. Jaffrelot, *Le Pakistan* (Paris: Fayard, 2000), p. 31.

29. *Ibid.*

30. According to Jaffrelot, it made progress between 1970 and 2000, *ibid.*, p. 67.

31. *Les Nationalistes hindous*, pp. 27, 82.

32. *Ibid.*, pp. 43, 58.

33. *Ibid.*, p. 87.

34. *Ibid.*, pp. 375, 397, 403.

35. This in no way justifies an identification between the first phase of decolonization of third-world countries and the second phase in Eastern Europe (after the fall of the Berlin wall), seen as a 'decolonization from socialism', contrary to what nationalists and ethnocrats from this region have claimed.

36. This is the case for nations and states as much as for groups. See *L'Inde contemporaine de 1950 à nos jours*, pp. 372 ff.

37. What was lacking in Yugoslavia was a clear concept of individual, citizenship, but exercised in common. One was not a Yugoslav citizen as a member of an ethnic group or a nation. The link between nationality and citizenship, which is always ambiguous, was particularly so in Yugoslavia. But the appearance of the term 'nationality' in all the questionnaires (in a concern for national 'secularism' and equidistance of identity) gave it a certain preponderance. A spirit of collectivity always rubbed off on the concept of citizenship, above and beyond its individual aspect, and made it difficult to separate out the individual, the common and the collective. This is an example of the (harmful) effects that theoretical confusion can have on political practice.

38. For example Austria-Hungary, according to István Bibó. 'When, at the end of the eighteenth century, modern democratic nationalism took off and staked its claim in Western and Northern Europe, there was no doubt that the framework the people wanted could only be national, and had to coincide with already-existing state borders (...) But the situation was not the same in Central and Eastern Europe. Two factors—the formation of the Germanic Holy Roman Empire and the invasion of the Ottoman empire—contributed to the formation of an empire which was to gravely compromise the constitution of national states in this region. This empire was that of the Habsburgs (...) No serious unification effort was to be observed in this conglomerate (...) Maria Theresa did not possess the title of empress, nor did her empire have a name; it was a congeries of nations and fragments of nations (...) Only in the second half of the eighteenth century did the desire to stimulate a vaguely 'Austrian' national consciousness spring up'. *Misère des petits Etats d'Eurape de l'Est* (Paris: Albin Michel, 1993), pp. 133–5.

39. R. Kumar, 'L'Inde: "Etat-nation" ou "Etat-civilization"?', in *Herodote*, No. 71, 'L' Inde et la question nationale', pp. 45–6.

40. The equivocation between the 'official' and the 'unofficial' was common in this system of semi-publicity. See R. Iveković, *Autopsia dei Balcani. Saggio di psico-politica* (Milan: Raffaello Cortina Editore, 1999).

41. One remark on the difficulty of perceiving origins-inspired violence, which extends to the possible analogies that might be drawn, I am referring to my own

experience of double blindness when, as a student of India, writing a doctoral dissertation there, I studied the painful history of partition, and observed the constant aggressiveness between the different communities. Firstly, I did not see any relationship between the two, and in any case this was officially hushed up. However, the origin of the phenomenon in violence guaranteed its essential principle and reproduced it, if only due to the necessity to justify partition as rational, and as having played a role in the founding of the nation, which, in the perspective of insane violence alone, made potential resistance to partition invisible. It is too often forgotten that partition is a continuous process which has continued up to our day, and will no doubt continue into the future. Secondly, as a young Yugoslav at the start of the 1970s, I did not draw any analogy with my own country, which, like India, was multi-national. The founding principles remain hidden from us. India, wisely, never adopted the doctrine of multiple nationalities following the original split, which amounted to tacitly admitting this division into two parts (while rejecting the theory of the two nations). The partition of India had already taken place, while that of Yugoslavia was still to come. After its occurrence, the analogies were, unfortunately, only too obvious.

42. Latinka Perović, *Ljudi, dogadjaji i knjige* (Belgrade: Helsinški odbor, 2000).

43. R. Samaddar, *The Marginal Nation*. See also Tapan K. Bose and Rita Manchanda (eds), *States, Citizens and Outsiders. The Uprooted People of South Asia* (Kathmandu: SAFHR, 1997).

44. R. Iveković, *Bénarès* (Paris: L'Harmattan, 2001).

45. The schema and legend in Figure 1 are taken from Renata Kodilja, 'identità nazionale e nazionalismo nell'ex-Jugoslavia. Un analisi psico-sociale', in G. Ieraci and L. Mattina (eds), *Studi Politici*, special issue devoted to Central, Eastern and Balkan Europe, p. 243. This schema applies to ex-Yugoslavia. We might point out that the author uses conventionally the term 'national identity' to talk about something that did not have the official status of a nation in that country; she uses the term 'identity of the state/republic' for what was officially considered as a nation. And it is precisely in this divergence between the official nomenclature and reality that the problem, not only theoretical but, in a real sense, practical, is situated. See Figure 2.

46. R. Iveković, 'Nation and Identity in Post-Socialist Transition', in K. Glass, R. Hettlage, and R. Scartezzini (eds), *Erweiterung Europas*, (Vienna; Poznań: Österr. Gesellschaft für Mitteleurop. Studien & Humaniora 1998), pp. 229–43.

47. Nebojša Popov, 'Disidentska skrivalica', *in Republika*, No. 242–3 (Belgrade, February 2000), p. 21.

48. J.-L. Racine, 'Rama et les joueurs de dés. Questions sur la nation indienne', *in Herodote*, No. 71, 'L'Inde et la question nationale', p. 20.

49. For the first few years after the second World War, Yugoslavia was strongly centralized, and organized along the lines of the Soviet model. The break between Tito and Stalin, in 1948, encouraged Yugoslavia to turn away from that particular

model. The rigidity of a regime with a totalitarian tendency gave way, little by little, to a system that was more flexible, less centralized, but at the same time organized round the party, and looser with regard to the relationship between the federation and the states. The sketched-out democracy was to be based on principles of self-management, in contradiction with the role of the party in bringing people together, and to the exclusion of other possible dimensions (for example, there was no room for the articulation of differences between the sexes in self-management). See Jože Pirjevec, *Serbi, croati, sloveni. Storia di tre nazioni* (Bologna: Il Mulino, 1995); also N. Popov, op. cit.

50. Partha Chatterjee, *The Nation and its Fragments: Colonial and Postcolonial Histories* (Princeton: Princeton University Press, 1993): A *Possible India Essays in Political Criticism* (Delhi: Oxford University Press, 1997); *The Partha Chatterjee Omnibus* (Delhi: Oxford University Press, 1999).

51. M. N. Srinivas, *The Dominant Caste and Other Essays* (Bombay/Calcutta, Madras: Oxford University Press, 1987); Veena Das, *Structure and Cognition* (Bombay/Calcutta/Madras: Oxford University Press, 1977); Dragoljub Nešić, 'Savremene promjene kastinskog poretka u selima Indije', in *Socijalno-etnička struktura i politički pokreti* (Belgrade: Institut za izučavanje radničkog pokreta, 1967). For the principle of the maintenance of identity, see my own publications.

52. In the social system of the four *varnas* (each of which consists of numerous castes), which leaves various pariahs, harijan, dalits, and untouchables in a state of invisibility, the term *brâhmana* (which designates an individual who belongs to a caste with sacred power) originates in the universalization of a principle and of a particular ideal which is dominant or hegemonic *(brahman)*, that is, that of the group's members. The subordination of the other castes has not always been experienced as oppressive, or a source of conflict, in any case not at every moment in history, since the interests of the brahmans can be espoused by all the others under the pretext of protection, and with the possibility of acquiring certain marketable assets. See R. Iveković, *Pregled indijske filozofije* (Zagreb: Filozofska misao, 1981). For a remarkable literary interpretation of a problem that concerns both caste relations, the relationship between the sexes as such, and the relationship between castes and gender differences in Kerala today, see Arundhati Roy, *The God of Small Things* (London: Flamingo/HarperCollins, 1997). See also *Esprit*, No. 107, 1985, special issue, 'La démocratie indienne', and notably Rajni Kothari's articles, as well as *Purushartha*, No. 16, 'Violence et nonviolence en Inde', 1994, notably the articles by M. Biardeau, Ch. Malamoud, and V. Das.

53. R. Iveković, *Druga Indija* (Zagreb: ŠK, 1982).

54. U. Butalia, 'The Margins', in *The Other Side of Silence*, pp. 223–58; Ritu Menon and Kamla Bhasin, *Borders & Boundaries. Women in India's Partition* (New Brunswick, N.J.: Rutgers University Press, 1998).

55. To the point where some authors (idealizing dangerously) talk about a

civilization-state rather than a nation-state, for example Ravinder Kumar, 'L' Inde. "Etat-nation" ou "Etat-civilization"?', in 'L' Inde et la question nationale', pp. 43–61. Further on, Jean-Alphonse Bernard writes that 'the events of 1946–1947 spelt the breakdown of a civilization-in-becoming in the name of a nation-state, as referred to by the two parties to the conflict' (ibid., p. 61). Max Jean Zins, in the same publication, applies another form of terminology: rather than talking about a civilization-state, he remarks that, 'faced with the concept of a nation-state, the Hindu nationalists refer to that of a nation-society. Here, of course, the individual finds his place, but only insofar as he is conceived of as being apart of a whole (...) and at the price of a certain depreciation of the concept of a state.' Ibid., p. 67.

56. Josip Županov, 'Tranzicija i politički kapitalizam', in Republika, November 1999, pp. 224–5. The author talks about 'political capitalism' (as opposed to 'economic' capitalism), but it is obvious that he is talking about symbolic capitalism, where 'capitalist values' have taken over on a global scale, within socialism as elsewhere.

57. Nationalism, having been discredited in Europe after 1945, found a new role in the framework of decolonization, and in the third world, 'manifesting analogies with the "awakening of the peoples" of Europe in the previous century, but also with an artful and more ingenious character', writes Francesco Tuccari in La nazione (Barr: Laterza, 2000), p. 130. Both can be either integrators or 'dismemberers'.

58. Partha Chatterjee, 'More on Modes of Power and the Peasantry', in R. Guha and G. Chakravorty Spivak (eds), Selected Subaltern Studies (New York/Oxford: Oxford University Press, 1988), p. 363.

59. Maurice Goldring, 'Irlande, droits collectifs et droits individuels', in M. Spensky (ed.), Universalisme, particularisme et citoyenneté dans les îles Britanniques, op. cit., p. 112.

60. Partha Chatterjee, 'More on Modes of Power and the Peasantry', in R. Guha and G. Chakravorty Spivak (eds), Selected Subaltern Studies, op. cit., pp. 351–90.

61. Jürgen Habermas, Die postnationole Konstellation. Politische Essays (Frankfurt a/ M.: Suhrkamp, 1998); quoted after the French translation. Après l'Etat-nation (Paris: Fayard, 2000), pp. 80–1.

62. Jashodhara Bagchi, 'Freedom in an Idiom of Loss: The Feminine in Partition literature and Cinema', in Alumnus. Presidency College Alumni Association, Autumn Annual, 1999, p. 53.

63. P. Chatterjee. 'The Nationalist Resolution of the Women's Question', in K. Sangari and S. Vaid (eds), Recasting Women. Essays in Indian Colonial History, op. cit., p. 244.

64. In the truncated Yugoslavia of the year 2000—a bankrupt country, prey to gangsters, where nothing was going right any more, on the eve of Milošević's umpteenth election—it seemed surprising that there was no non-nationalist resis-

tance. The fact is that it existed as a potentiality, but was not (sufficiently) organized, and could not find expression or acceptance in a situation where the regime and the 'opposition' took up the entire public space, in a process which included monopolizing the attention of well-intentioned foreign observers, who accordingly adopted the prevailing discourse. This was a country in which it was not just the power structure that needed to be changed, but also the 'opposition', whose effect had masked, or indeed precluded, all resistance, having usurped its rightful terrain.

65. See R. Samaddar, 'The Last Hurrah That Continues', in this volume.

PORTRAIT

Jerusalem's Stumbling Blocks*

ANTOINE MAURICE

Entering Jerusalem from the east is in itself a political choice. Mentioning the West Bank is another; one which conjures up the now dated negotiations of the Oslo process and the Security Council resolutions. Those resolutions themselves, referring both to occupied territories and Palestinian territories, also offer a choice. Coming from the Allenby Bridge and Jericho, travellers can choose to make their way along the back roads which unexpectedly end up behind the Mount of Olives, providing an entirely different relationship to the metropolis: the perspective, that is, of the Palestinians, when they make their way into the old city through the service entrance when a blockade of the territories is in effect. Winding roads, incredible in how they negotiate the hills and valleys, the thousand-year-old network where donkeys plod along bearing water and peasants make their way to market.

The entrance from the west is, on the other hand, entirely modern, and is principally along highway number 1—a large strip of highway that leads to Tel Aviv and serves as the Israeli state's main artery. The west side is made up of neighbourhoods in dormitory towns, their buildings made from the white stone of Jerusalem with right angles and windows as narrow as arrow-slits, solar panels on the roofs, and malls in the midst of immense parking lots. In this way, one gets to Jaffa Road and the Jerusalem of the nineteenth and twentieth centuries, where a number of perpendicular roads intersect.

Thus, the agglomeration is immediately divided not in two, but rather into three: the fortress neighbourhoods of greater Jerusalem, stifling the Palestinian villages, and the Israeli city. The old city, finally, floats like a ship

* Translated from the French by Stephen Wright

upon the seas of this torn territory, with its religious and no-longer state-specific quarters: Muslim, Jewish, Armenian Christian. More than a brief tourist visit is required to discover that this division is not a peaceful cohabitation but a rift engraved in the stone itself. The dynamics resemble those of the virgin vine which climbs the walls of a house, squeezing it little by little in a merciless corset, devouring the structure's very substance.

It is also on the periphery that the moving equilibrium of the offensive and the defensive can be measured. Time was needed—practically all the way to the collapse of the Oslo process—for it to be possible to look at this biblical landscape in its new prophetic configuration. To see the new Israeli cities on the hillsides for what they are—that is, as strategic extensions of the territories in the east, beyond the 1967 line. As extensions inscribed in the organic road and real-estate network of the Israeli city in its full metropolitan appetite. Relationships to the land are not the same: urban and security-oriented on the Israeli side, rural on the Palestinian side. Though the hold on the land changes, the passion is identical, and both sides lay claim to the geography as if it were their own, with its acres of loose stones and the rare patch of arable land in the hollows. 'This land is our land' proclaim the buildings of the settlements, imperious as castles. Or, as Frédéric Encel notes with regard to the Palestinians:[1] 'nothing that our fathers passed on to us will change'.

Laurent arrived in Israel after 1968. Of French origin, his *Aliya*[2] came in the midst of the wave of upheavals of the sixties, when he was twenty years old. He moved to Jerusalem, got married, had two children who are completely Israeli. He has kept something of the wandering Jew, as he is only too happy to acknowledge, and which he attributes to his French, Bulgarian, and Spanish origins. He remains attached to Europe where his work as a journalist often takes him. His relationship to the holy city is ambiguous. He does not have the slightest religious fibre in him, Jewish or otherwise. It was not so much Jerusalem that attracted him; it was more that it requisitioned him. He was in need of retraining, and Israeli politics sought to push new emigrants toward the reunified city. He lives in a central, modern, Israeli quarter, well-off and well-appointed, without going overboard. His work takes up all his time, but he likes to take his friends down along the walls or up to one of the panoramic viewpoints onto the west, where the light descends from the sky as if it were an emergency vehicle. Jerusalem, he admits, is a tense and rather inhospitable city. With the exception of the Orthodox Jews and the employees of the three religions, many Israelis would rather live on the coastal plain. They nevertheless share with Laurent something of the pride of pioneers for this reunification adventure which they have managed to bring about. This mixture of the strategic and the spiritual is unique. It provokes both admiration and malaise.

The relationship to Jerusalem's space—not only to the land—is tiresome because it is forever mobilising the individual both in the spiritual and the strategic realms. In Jerusalem, war pursues religion and urbanizing by other means. What gives off a feeling of malaise in the city has to do with the debauchery of aesthetic admiration and spiritual fervour regarding the petty-minded self-interest of predatory advances and retreats on the ground. It is an explosive mixture, coming from the three Bookbased religions, all three of which hold goodness and social tolerance as a common value. Jerusalem is so charged with tensions that this value cannot be experienced without that form of religious hypocrisy known as bigotry. Laurent suggested this disenchantment even as he showed me the at once intimate and breathtaking panorama, which spreads out beneath the public gardens (the Haas Promenade) on the road to Bethlehem.

At the beginning of the peace process, Sari Nusseibeh received me in his house near the American Colony Hotel, near the green line and the highway which has replaced it to feed the Israeli space and the fortress cities conquered from the enemy. In Europe, fortresses were footholds for consolidating the territories they had acquired in the middle east; since the Crusades, they have remained a door to be bolted shut in the face of the enemy's advance. Nusseibeh's mother received us in traditional Palestinian dress, a scarf on her head. She speaks perfect English; her husband was a high official at the time of the British mandate and the Jordanian administration. In 1948, they stayed behind, just as they did once again in 1967. Their family home is a building of good proportions, constructed at the beginning of the century in Jerusalem stone. In the city's Palestinian quarters, generally situated lower down and well shaded, the stone takes on a shade of grey which only becomes white or golden in the evening light. Nusseibeh, an academic, took part in the Madrid process and was a member of the team of intellectuals from within who were part of Arafat's circle. Several months after our meeting, he jointly published a book with an Israeli intellectual—which caused a considerable stir—about peace and how to attain it. We often worked in this house, he said, in the middle of this bourgeois quarter of the east, which is so calm and peaceful in its sleepy urbanism.

Of the two intellectuals, it was Nusseibeh who had to go into exile to teach at Oxford. The decision was a professional one, but when, in his capacity as a political scientist, he was explaining the situation to me, I came to understand that there was no place for him either in the Palestinian authority or in academic co-operation with Israeli and Arab intellectuals. The cordoning off of the territories, which was so frequent at the time and has now become virtually permanent, approaches the feeling of exclusion from their own land that American Indians must feel on their reserves or that the Blacks in the homelands must have felt under apartheid in South Africa; interior exile, with an escape hatch through immigration for the better educated. The hell of sainthood.

The lovers of the old stones of this Mont-Saint-Michel lying on its side— which is one way of looking at the Wailing Wall—take advantage of the early morning hours, after the opening of the gates, at a time when the setting of commercial and religious ambushes is just getting underway because the Palestinians—with the exception of those who actually live in the old city— are not allowed in before the gates are opened. The shops get their deliveries on small hand trolleys; buckets of water are sloshed over the ground to wash it; patrons sit down for a tea or coffee on the still-quiet terraces, where adept waiters—like the local taxi drivers—are only too pleased to show off their political science. The city's multiple layers of sound awaken: the chanting of the merchants, litanies of the Jewish schools, and Byzantine liturgies of the Christians echo one another from one landing, one storey to the next.

The inside walls, cleft with narrow, barred windows, are a precaution to preserve meditation and prayer in the Armenian quarter. The walls delimit an interlacing of minorities at once confronted with and leaning against one another. Walls, storeys, and deceptive half-storeys all make for a piling-up of religious establishments whose surface space is multiplied still further underground. Which is why the digging of a tunnel in 1997 beneath the Esplanade of the Mosques immediately took on the proportions of an evasion-invasion into the underground of the other. Both sides flee, and in their movement invade and threaten their neighbour. Digging goes on, as Elias Sanbar, editor of the *Revue d'Etudes palestiniennes*, has noted, to prove seniority on the site. The past is measured vertically, and the only reply to the other community's digging is to dig deeper still. To which is added the labyrinthine passageways, the stone trenches and other gullies which block off pedestrian traffic, or else channel it toward stairways that can be kept under surveillance, surrounding walls and secondary walls. Everyone tries at once to remain isolated from the pedestrian public, to close themselves off from the adversary religion and to launch a counter-encirclement.

In this old city, dominated by the double impregnation of commerce and a war of attrition, visitors are invited to walk along without getting lost, in well-grouped packages, without dawdling even in the shops along the Via dolorosa so as not to create bottlenecks; without disturbing, except through their alms, the pathetic balance of the Christian holy places, which cultivate an ancient rancour around the tomb of Christ. They have to move along, and keep moving along, lose their sense of the east and the west through the tortuous alleyways, finally ending up at the Wailing Wall. Alas, the zealots' fervour does not stem from brotherhood; rather, their devotion beneath the ultimate rampart at the foot of the Wall refers to the unparalleled antiquity of Jewish monotheism. On the Esplanade of the Mosques, the largest flat space in Jerusalem, there are always people. Believers, especially on Friday. People come and go beneath the gilded dome, as if at the entrance to a hive in which non-Muslims are not allowed. As soon as things heat up, the tension becomes palpable, the Esplanade fills up with young demonstrators whereas the Israeli police deploys all around. The Mosque overlooks the Wailing Wall, where the Palestinians enjoy one of their few dominant positions and the Israeli's tactic is to attack them from behind and from further above. In ordinary times—if that means anything at all in Jerusalem—the centre of Islam displays a stable and somewhat timeless serenity, characteristic of places of worship devoted to prayer and meditation.

The visitor can feel a malaise as the ancient mortared stones exude antipathy rather than human brotherhood—a sort of *turista* of the soul, which might be referred to as the 'Jerusalem Syndrome'. Of course, proverbs and pontiffs of the three religions—like the Pope last year—resoundingly evoke a reconciled humanity. Yet this humanism, tirelessly and fondly kindled by the clerics in residence, is cold comfort against the petrifaction of accumulated hatred and history, so tragically manifest in the brutal failure of the Oslo peace process. All the more so given that, outside, the figure of Greater Jerusalem reproduces the features of an urbanism of contention and Israeli expansion, at the expense of the Palestinian lands and populations. The fortress cities surround Jerusalem like sentinels, while safe, high-speed expressways run from the core toward the peripheries where the settlements are built. Bit by bit, the Palestinians figured out what was really at stake beneath the Oslo cloak—that is, not the freeze but rather the accentuation of a strategy of Israeli encroachment on Palestine. The rise of widespread

Palestinian resentment, regardless of the form of political organization one detects within it, is founded on nothing other than a resurgence of frustration, born of the spectacle of a country in the throws of strangulation. And nowhere is this more obvious than in Jerusalem.

For the better part of the day, light impassively floods this theatre of divided stones, quarters, embankments, levels, and ghosts, becoming oblique toward the end of its arc, when its mildness brings thoughts to everyone's mind of escape and the promise of repose. It is the hour when the merchants fold up their wares and shut their iron curtains, and the old city empties out with a sort of palpable slackening of tension—not least of all amongst the Israeli soldiers on duty. The light streams more than it bathes. It emphasizes through the rare clouds its immutable verticality. It links, of course, the earth with the heavens, but apart from this vertical religion which occupies so many men and women in their day-to-day lives, the light it casts on the compartments of the city reaches right to the very bottom of the trenches, emphasizing walls great and small, outlining the axes of communication, highlighting the modern, wilful lines of modern planning. It is always noon in Jerusalem, because the people, as if in a sort of upside-down Babel—built from the pinnacles of the minarets toward the buried naves—come to life with their backs to one another rather than side by side. When, finally moving from its zenith, the light declines into the western sky, a feeling of relief fills bodies and souls. It announces a respite but also the forever recommencing impossibility of overcoming divisions other than in the twilit reveries and the sleep of utopias.

Obsessions of identity ooze from the Jerusalem stone, which in the declining light takes on the exquisite taints of sacred painting. As has been the case for painters since the Middle Ages, one need only to have travelled there in order to change class with regard to one's contemporaries. The process—like that of pilgrims to Mecca or Lourdes—denotes a sort of spiritual snobbishness. By walking on the Palestinian soil, one enters into the circle of the hadji, of the chosen; one draws slightly nearer to the beyond. Despite the ecumenical or Scandinavian dreams of Oslo, what is once again at issue is an identity as cruel as it is exclusive: I cannot be me except insofar as the other cannot be. Palestinian by antiquity, Israeli by the same title, and Christian because it was here that God consummated his alliance with men. In short, hatred reigns here as the flip-side of a much heralded love, which remains obstinately inaccessible.

The mutual rhetoric of war clings to the eloquence of the buildings. The Israelis proffer their constant warning: 'this time we did not strike because we are watching out for you (we love you)', even as they crush the Palestinians beneath bullets and rockets. The Palestinians. on the other hand, envelop themselves in a national pride that grows ever more narcissistic and murderous as the reality of might demeans them still further. Jerusalem, meanwhile, in its deceptively suave faith, drowned in its pathology of verticality, suffers a terrible repudiation that neither incense nor prayers can remedy.

Notes

1. In *Géopolitique de Jérusalem* (Paris: Flammarion, 1998).

2. *Aliya* is an individual political decision by means of which the Jews of the Diaspora move to Israel on the basis of political or religious conviction to live in the land of their ancestors.

3. Marc A. Heller, Sari Nusseibeh, *No Trumpets no Drums, a two-state settlement of the Israeli-Palestinian conflict* (New York: Hill and Wang ,1991).

Contributors

RADHA KUMAR is a Senior Fellow for Peace and Conflict Studies at the Council on Foreign Relations in New York, where she directs the Council's Project on Ethnic Conflict, Partition, and Post-Conflict Reconstruction.

RANABIR SAMADDAR is director of the Peace Studies programme at the South-Asia Forum for Human Rights, Kathmandu, and former professor at the Maulana Abul Kalam Azad Institute of Asian Studies, Kolkata. His work has been in the fields of labour studies, postcolonial nationalism in South Asia, and migration and refugee studies.

FRIEDRICH DIECKMANN, born in 1937, writer and essayist, lives in Berlin-Treptow. From 1972 to 1976 he was a dramaturge with the Berliner Ensemble, and in 1989–90 fellow at the Wissenschaftskolleg in Berlin. Vice-president of the Academy of Fine Arts of Saxony, he is rapporteur of the Deutsche Literaturkonferenz e. V., a member of the German Academy of the Arts (Darmstadt), the Independent Academy of Fine Arts of Leipzig, the Academy of Fine Arts of Berlin-Brandenburg, and the International PEN Club.

CLAUDE MARKOVITS is director of research at the CNRS.

JACQUES RUPNIK is director of research at the Centre for International Studies and Research, at the National Political Science Foundation, Paris. He was the executive director of the International Commission on the Balkans, whose report, entitled *Unfinished Peace*, was published in 1996.

GORAN FEJIĆ, an economist, was a diplomat in the former Yugoslavia; he resigned in 1991, in a refusal to support the war. He went into exile in Paris, and has recently participated in his personal capacity in a number of UN peace missions (Haiti, South Africa, Guatemala, and Afghanistan).

SYED SIKANDER MEHDI is Professor and Chairman of the Department of International Relations at the University of Karachi, Pakistan.

MEGHNA GUHATHAKURTA is professor in the Department of International Relations, University of Dhaka, Bangladesh. Her fields of specialisation are South-Asian politics, development and gender studies. She is associate editor of *The Journal of Social Studies*, a quarterly journal of social science published in Dhaka. She has written extensively on the women's movement, development politics in Bangladesh and family histories of the Partition.

OZREN KEBO born in Mostar, has spent most of his life in Sarajevo. He is a journalist with *Dani*.

AHMET ALTAN has struggled in favour of democracy, and was the editorialist for the daily centre left newspaper *Milliyet* and he has published several best-selling novels, which have sold more than 100,000 copies in Turkey.

RITU MENON is a publisher and independent scholar. She lives in New Delhi. She has written extensively on women and violence, women and media, and women in conflict. She is currently working on an all India study of the social and economic status of Muslim women in India.

SUBHORANJAN DASGUPTA is professor at the School of Women's Studies, Jadavpur University, Kolkata.

MUSHIRUL HASAN is Professor of History at Jamia Millia Islamia University, New Delhi.

RADA IVEKOVIĆ is Professor in philosophy at the University of Saint Etienne, France.

ANTOINE MAURICE is a journalist with the *La Tribune de Genève* and professor of communication sciences at the University of Neuchâtel.

Index